THOMAS HARDY'S EPIC-DRAMA: A STUDY OF *THE DYNASTS*

THOMAS HARDY'S EPIC-DRAMA:
A STUDY OF *THE DYNASTS*

by

Harold Orel

UNIVERSITY OF KANSAS PRESS
LAWRENCE, 1963

PRINTED IN THE U.S.A. BY THE
UNIVERSITY OF KANSAS PRESS
LAWRENCE, KANSAS

TO M. D. W.

Preface

THIS BOOK was written because of my admiration for Thomas Hardy's *The Dynasts*, and because of my feeling that the last word has not yet been said about it.

What I want to do is reëmphasize the meaning behind Hardy's descriptive epithet, "epic-drama." To that end, I have retraced Hardy's career up to the moment he renounced the writing of novels and became a full-time poet. Poetry, for Hardy, was always the highest form of art; it was the kind of literature he wanted most to create. For years he had been contemplating a large work, a poem on the epic scale, which he needed time to write. It may be no exaggeration to say that his entire life led up to *The Dynasts*, and that for him it represented the supreme artistic work of his career.

Since *The Dynasts* has often been considered primarily in terms of its philosophy, although Hardy declared vehemently on several occasions that his poem should be judged on artistic grounds, it has seemed worthwhile to reëxamine the views that Hardy held on the nature of the universe and whatever gods exist. They were not radical or even unusual beliefs for the late Victorian era. Hardy's "pessimism" was shared by many of his most eminent contemporaries, and, as I try to show, he did not need to borrow major features of it from German philosophy. At any rate, a consideration of his own views enables us to judge how accurately they are reflected by the speeches of the Spirits in *The Dynasts*.

The Dynasts does not resemble completely the epics of earlier centuries; yet it shares with them a world-view, a sense that the deeds of men have some relationship to the Spirits who dwell in the vast reaches of time and space. It is, like them, a poem of sublime aspect. The elements which contribute to that sublimity were clearly defined by Edmund Burke, and Hardy, who had studied Burke's aesthetics, was deliberately using them for literary effect.

The discussion of Hardy and the sublime, however, is prologue to an even more important consideration: the ways in which *The Dynasts* modifies or renounces conventions of the one epic with which it (and Hardy) invited comparison, namely, Milton's *Paradise Lost.* I believe that *The Dynasts* proposes three new ways of looking at ourselves and the role we play in this "earth-tragedy."

Finally, to illustrate the anti-heroic temper of Hardy's epic-drama, I have compared Homer's ambivalent attitude toward war with Hardy's forthright denunciation of it as a principle for settling international disputes. Although the *Iliad* does not glorify killing, the view of *arete* that it promotes had become, for Hardy, too dangerous to be supported in a twentieth-century epic.

Through *The Dynasts* a noble voice speaks. The poem is, indeed, one of the glorious achievements of English literature, and a reconsideration of its affinities to the great epics of the past may help us to assess more truly the magnitude of Hardy's achievement.

This study had its genesis in an article I wrote some years ago, which was printed in the *South Atlantic Quarterly* in July, 1953. That article (copyright, 1953, by the Duke University Press) forms the basis of Chapter Five, "*The Dynasts* and *Paradise Lost*," and I should like to thank Mr. W. B. Hamilton, Managing Editor, for permission to quote from it.

I am also grateful to the Trustees of the Hardy Estate and to Macmillan & Co. Ltd. for permission to make a film of the manuscript of *The Dynasts* (Additional 38183-5), and to the Keeper of the Department of Manuscripts in the British Museum for his kind coöperation.

To the Editor of the University of Kansas Press, I express my deepest thanks for his careful and sympathetic criticism. The generous help of the University Research Committee at the University of Kansas is also much appreciated.

And to all the scholars and critics who have admired Thomas Hardy, and who have written so ably about his works, I am indebted far beyond my capacity to repay. All scholarship builds on what has gone before, and, in Robert Herrick's phrase, "He pays the half, who does confess the debt."

—H. O.

Contents

CHAPTER ONE

Prologue to a Poet's Career: 1868-1896

FOR A FULL understanding of the reasons that led Thomas Hardy to write *The Dynasts* relatively late in his career, we must review the problems that Hardy faced in making his prose fictions acceptable to his Victorian audience. A work written late in a man's career may not necessarily be better than the works of his youth, but I hope to demonstrate, briefly because so much of this matter is familiar to Hardy students, that a lifetime of preparation preceded the composition of this particular work; and my ultimate intention is to show, convincingly if possible, that *The Dynasts* is Hardy's poetic testament, the work of his ripest years and judgment.

To begin, then, at the beginning, with Hardy's first published novel, *Desperate Remedies* (1871): it appeared anonymously because Hardy still was attempting to develop his professional career as an architect. One of its chapters had been cannibalized from a previously unsuccessful novel-manuscript, which Hardy had entitled *The Poor Man and the Lady*. Of the art of *Desperate Remedies*, little that is commendatory may be said; the plot is occasionally wild and strained, and even if individual sentences have the poetic flavor of their author, a man who used to notice such things as "the passed-away fortunes of the Three Tranters Inn," the whole is apprentice work. But Hardy's earnest, even humorless imitation of Wilkie Collins suggests that he had taken a close look at the kind of novel that would sell. The fact that Hardy's novel was submitted to, and published by, Tinsley Brothers, the firm which had published *The Moonstone* in 1868, is suggestive in itself.

Hardy had learned something from his experiences in attempting to sell *The Poor Man and the Lady*. Alexander Macmillan, for example, had told him that he exaggerated unreasonably the "frivolity, heartlessness, selfishness" of the London aristocracy, and that he might do well to consider the lighter bantering tone which Thackeray had used in scoring the same points; that improbabilities might seem more acceptable to a reading audience if they occurred in foreign countries or came "from old books"; and that, in general, the air of contrivance settled too heavily over crucial plot details. Hardy was more than willing to "consider" Macmillan's suggestions; he traveled to London in December, 1868, to talk about them; and even if that visit turned out to be useful primarily as a means of meeting another publisher, Hardy's determination to benefit by the advice of professionals shows up clearly in this matter. Perhaps the most useful advice came from George Meredith, who warned him about the likelihood that publication of the manuscript would damage his reputation, and who suggested either diluting the social satire or shelving the novel in favor of another, and more complicated, novel with more promising commercial possibilities.

Desperate Remedies, the second-try manuscript, sold poorly as a three-decker; but even if comparisons with *The Poor Man and the Lady* are risky because so much of the manuscript was destroyed by Hardy in later years (exactly what happened to it is a bibliographical mystery), our guess that his first published novel was superior to his first written novel seems reasonable enough. Superior, in other words, in the sense that Meredith had hoped it might be: as a salable commodity, if not to the general public, to the publisher in a position to accept or reject it.

Under the Greenwood Tree (1872), also published anonymously, explored more fully the rustic dialogue and behavior which Alexander Macmillan had found praiseworthy in the unlamented manuscript of *The Poor Man and the Lady*. The idyll of Fancy Day, the schoolmistress, and Dick Dewy, was a lovely story: uncomplicated, pastoral in the best sense, and shrewdly humorous. Yet its appealing *wholeness* as a story—Fancy Day is engaged to one man, promises to marry another, decides not to reveal her promise to her original fiancé—should not make us forget that its first eight chapters came over relatively intact from *The Poor Man and the Lady*. Hardy was learning one lesson well: an artist should never throw out a manuscript until he has exploited its possibilities in as many ways as possible.

Leslie Stephen's approbation and Tinsley's enthusiasm, nevertheless, were insufficient to elevate *Under the Greenwood Tree* to the status of a best-seller. It is true that Henry Holt published the novel under Hardy's name in the United States (1873), and that the novel had a number of pirated editions in this country; but the disappointment that Hardy experienced when he thought of its English reception led to his taking a step with serious consequences for his development as an artist. He agreed to a proposal made by his well-intentioned publisher: to write a novel which would appear, in evenly spaced installments, in *Tinsleys' Magazine*. His desire to renounce architecture, his natural interest in enhancing his reputation and increasing his income, and his eagerness to justify Tinsley's faith in his abilities, make understandable the move. An adjustment to the ways of magazine publishers would have been inevitable, anyhow, given the conditions of publication which prevailed in the 1870's, and Hardy's next novel, *A Pair of Blue Eyes*, which ran in *Tinsleys' Magazine* from September, 1872, to July, 1873, represented in some ways significant progress in his narrative art. Hardy also had the pleasure of seeing his name printed on the title-page of the novel (1873), for the first time in an English edition.

Again Hardy used some manuscript material from *The Poor Man and the Lady*. Again, too, he reproduced the speech of laborers with uncanny fidelity, perhaps most brilliantly in the gravediggers' scene (Chapter xxvi, prefaced by the tag, "To that last nothing under earth"), with its distinction between the law of the living—"a man shall be upright and downright"—and the law of the dead—"a man shall be east and west." And a novel which could win the admiration of William Dean Howells,

3

Coventry Patmore, and Alfred Tennyson is not necessarily the worse for having made a first appearance in a periodical. Yet Hardy's admiration of Gothic elements of story-telling, his honest wish to please an audience with each installment, and his interest in coincidences, reversals, and the element of chance were stimulated to an unfortunate degree by what for him was a new mode of publication. One may well ask whether the train ride to Cornwall, taken by Stephen Smith and Henry Knight together in the company of the dead Elfride, would have been so devised if the novel had not come out first as a serial.

Leslie Stephen, as the next figure in the drama, wanted Hardy's new novel for the *Cornhill Magazine*, and it is significant of the new fever in Hardy's blood that, as in the case of *A Pair of Blue Eyes*, publication of the first installment began before the whole manuscript had been completed. *Far from the Madding Crowd* (1874) was his first popular success, and ran through seven editions during its first year; on the basis of Hardy's confidence in the future, now guaranteed by best-sellerdom, he married Emma Lavinia Gifford (September 17, 1874) and toured France on his honeymoon. It was altogether a world of promise, of greater and more resounding successes waiting on the horizon.

But the fact that Hardy's fictions now were signed meant that readers who disliked anything on the printed page knew where they might direct their criticisms. The delegation of Americans who protested against his description of the stoning of a dog did so at Hardy's home. Subscribers to *Cornhill Magazine* had moralistic objections to what they considered coarse or offensive passages, and Leslie Stephen, who at first shocked Hardy with his warning about the need for care in describing Fanny Robin's fall from grace, had his way: Hardy's treatment of the matter, so far as the periodical was concerned, observed the rules of decorum.

It is not the intention of this introductory sketch to trace Hardy's development as an artist, but rather (in part) to show that that development was significantly affected by the tastes and prejudices of a reading audience unprepared to appreciate his contribution to candor in English fiction. Now there was a grittiness about Hardy, even from the beginning, which we can only admire. Moreover, Hardy's compromises were sometimes good for the health of the manuscript, and later revisions, made for book publication, showed a tough-minded professional at work; they went beyond undoing the damage made by Grundyism, and improved the narrative in important ways. A full study of the changes made in the various versions of his novels will undoubtedly document the conclusion, drawn from the textual investigation of some selected novels, that Hardy's final, approved "Wessex Edition" published by Macmillan (1912) was carefully edited by the author himself, and represents the best text; in some cases, it is the only text that reliably reflects his intentions.

But the cost in nervous strain, misunderstandings, recriminations, time-devouring correspondence, and unpleasantness drained Hardy's energies, embittered his love of novel-writing, and led to his renunciation of the craft some two decades after the appearance of *Far from the Madding Crowd*. His next novel, written to satisfy Leslie Stephen's request for a second novel for the *Cornhill*, indicated the unfortunate nature of the influence that could be exerted on an author anxious to satisfy an audience rather than his own sense of what was artistically fitting. *The Hand of Ethelberta*, published in book form in 1876, was, in Hardy's own words, a "somewhat frivolous narrative," and its obsession with the opinions of servants endeared it neither to Mrs. Hardy nor to the public. Hardy had written it to show that he imitated no writer (the charge had been made against him on the basis of fancied similarities between *Far from the Madding Crowd* and the narratives of George Eliot), and that his range of interests was wider than had been popularly assumed. But his primary concern lay in a foredoomed guessing-game (what would his readers like?), and he undertook a description of drawing-room society that could convince readers of its authenticity only if the author had known a great deal more about the milieu.

The first major statement of Hardy's stern outlook on life, shaped at least partially by readings in post-Darwinian science, appeared in *The Return of the Native*, which was published in serial form in *Belgravia* in 1878. But the reason that Leslie Stephen did not publish the finished work in the *Cornhill* had little to do with distaste of doctrine. Stephen, who had disliked the suggestion of "the very close embrace in the London churchyard"[1] in *The Hand of Ethelberta*, had serious premonitions, after reading the opening chapters of an early version of *The Return of the Native*, "that the relations between Eustacia, Wildeve, and Thomasin might develop into something 'dangerous' for a family magazine, and he refused to have anything to do with it unless he could see the whole."[2] Hardy's arrangement with Chatto and Windus, publisher of *Belgravia*, had followed directly afterwards, and, as might well be expected when ten out of the twelve installments yet remained to be written, the exigencies of periodical publication again operated balefully.

John Paterson, in his study of the unique manuscript of the novel (now at the Library of the University College, Dublin), has shown that this was no more than a rough draft for the printers; that Hardy painstakingly went over the proof sheets and revised them extensively; that in 1878 a crucial series of changes were made for publication by Smith, Elder and Company; that in 1895 still another revision was made for the inclusion of the novel as Volume VI of the Uniform Edition, published by Osgood, McIlvaine, and Company (and later by Harper's); and that in 1912 one last editing was undertaken for the Wessex Edition, issued by Macmillan.[3] In Hardy's first plan, the original version (which Paterson calls the "Ur-novel") would have made no provision for Thomasin and Venn to marry; Thomasin would have continued her widowhood, and Venn would have vanished from Egdon Heath. Diggory Venn's marriage was wryly excused in later years by Hardy: "Readers can choose between the endings, and those with an austere artistic code can assume the more consistent conclusion to be the true one." Moreover, it is naïve to expect that the editors of *Belgravia* would be less concerned about the moral safety of their readers than Leslie Stephen was for the audience of subscribers to the *Cornhill*: for the pages of *Belgravia* Wildeve became more innocent and less philandering, Eustacia a good deal less of a supernatural being, the hostile allusions to Christianity were toned down, and the language was consistently bowdlerized. "How far this finicky censorship circumscribed the free imaginative development of the novel cannot of course be gauged at this point," Paterson concluded. "Everything suggests, however, that it wrought an ultimately irreparable damage and, more particularly, that it made impossible an honest representation of the relations between Wildeve and Eustacia."[4]

Add, finally, the failure of Hardy's contemporaries to see that *The Return of the Native* represented a major step forward for the novelist of pastoral idylls; that this, in fact, was his finest work. The reviews suggested the existence of "some artificiality," censured the "uncommonly slow" movement of the narrative, and even alleged the existence of some parodic intent.[5] It was all unjust (the *Athenaeum* questioned even the authenticity of his rustic dialogue), and more than a little depressing to a writer who read his reviews as carefully as Hardy did.

The Trumpet-Major, completed in 1879 and published the following year, is interesting primarily because of its connection with the Napoleonic Wars. The painstaking research that Hardy expended upon writing it bore richer fruit when he came to *The Dynasts*. Hence, it will be discussed later in this study. It was, at any rate, not one of his better novels, and is not often read today. But its serialization in *Good Words* had not ended before Hardy, under contract to write *A Laodicean* for Harper and Brothers at

£100 an installment, which in turn would be published in the European edition of *Harper's New Monthly Magazine,* became involved in the kind of crisis that writers like Dickens and Dostoyevsky had known before him. With only three installments completed (some thirteen chapters), and printing already under way, Hardy collapsed with internal bleeding.[6] A major operation was put off only because he promised his doctor to lie in bed for several months. During this enforced immobility he dictated the remainder of the text to Mrs. Hardy. The wretchedness of this particular novel, which has led some readers to pronounce it Hardy's least distinguished effort, was intensified by the determination of its author to complete it under the most painful and unpromising of circumstances. But in admiring his courage, we are also bound to remember that Hardy's decision to persevere had nothing to do with an inner conviction that this story of Miss Paula Power and George Somerset, despite its reliance on Hardy's memories of his training as a professional architect, *had* to be told. He "felt determined to finish the novel, at whatever stress to himself"—so Hardy wrote later, in the pertinent passage of his autobiography—"so as not to ruin the new venture of the publishers, and also in the interests of his wife, for whom as yet he had made but a poor provision in the event of his own decease."[7]

It is, of course, unfair to censure Hardy for writing for his bread; but magazine serialization offered little opportunity for taking time with each composition; for rewriting; for being sure that this was what he wanted to say. *Two on a Tower,* published in the *Atlantic Monthly* (1881), was still another disappointment to his admirers, and, more important, to Hardy himself. He wrote to Edmund Gosse on January 21, 1883: "The truth is that, though the plan of the story was carefully thought out, the actual writing was lamentably hurried—having been produced month by month, and the MS. despatched to America, where it was printed without my seeing the proofs. It would have been rewritten for the book form if I had not played truant and gone off to Paris."[8] Readers were more dismayed by matters of morality than of art. Lady Constantine's trick on Bishop Helmsdale, whom she married while already pregnant with another man's child, roused some readers to object to Hardy's "satire"; and Hardy, in turn, felt himself obliged to deny that he had intended any insult to the Church, even if, as was undeniably the case, the Bishop had been victimized in the story.[9] The Bishop, Hardy argued, was "every inch a gentleman."

Fortunately, Hardy's work on Max Gate, into which he moved on June 29, 1885, kept him so busy that he was able to set into proper perspective the adverse criticisms of *Two on a Tower*. His next novel, *The Mayor of Casterbridge*, written for the most part in 1884, reflected his maturing wisdom, and showed that he could produce literature when not harried by the recurring crises of magazine publication. This novel was completed on April 17, 1885; a complete set of proofs were ready by October 20; and the first published installment did not appear in the *Graphic* until January, 1886.

The novel was, and is, one of Hardy's supreme successes; and the revisions made before publication by Smith, Elder & Co., particularly in five chapters (12, 18, 34, 43, and 44), were further evidence of the care that Hardy could lavish on a narrative when blessed by adequate time. Some sensationalism remained, nevertheless, and Hardy judged it harshly: "It was a story which Hardy fancied he had damaged more recklessly as an artistic whole, in the interest of the newspaper in which it appeared serially, than perhaps any other of his novels, his aiming to get an incident into almost every week's part causing him in his own judgment to add events to the narrative somewhat too freely."[10] But Hardy generally believed that his novels were "mere journey-work," and protested late in life that he had never wanted to write prose novels at all: "Circumstances compelled me to turn them out."[11] Hence, some modification of Hardy's severe assessment seems necessary, and certainly other readers—Robert Louis Stevenson and Gerard Manley Hopkins, for example—greatly admired the book. The revisions which Hardy made for Osgood, McIlvaine's edition of the Wessex Novels (1895) "at the instance of some good judges across the Atlantic" (more specifically, Rebekah and Catharine Owen, of New York City[12]) restored those portions of Chapter 44 which discussed Henchard's visitation to Elizabeth-Jane's wedding and the death of the caged goldfinch; also, some corrections of Mr. Farfrae's Scotticisms were made; these were not concessions to satisfy indignant moralists, but, rather, alterations which strengthened the artistic wholeness and accuracy of the text.

With *The Woodlanders*, a much under-appreciated novel even today, Hardy again took his time. In its final form the book pleased him more than any of his other works. It appeared in *Macmillan's Magazine* between May, 1886, and April, 1887, and was published by Macmillan in March, some five weeks after he finished writing the last installment (February 4). The final number of pirated American editions (nineteen, all of them based on the uncorrected text which had appeared in *Harper's Bazaar*) signified the extent of Hardy's popularity overseas and the eagerness of unscrupulous publishers to cash in on it; but the text in its magazine form was only the first of *five* versions, and by far the least reliable, a fact which explains the relative lack of enthusiasm among American readers for *The Woodlanders*. Not until 1958, when Carl J. Weber edited the first American textbook edition for Harper's Modern Classics, did the version printed in the Macmillan Wessex Edition of 1912 become available in this country.

The revisions of *The Woodlanders* afford more evidence (although none is needed) that Hardy knew very well how to polish his text. He would lavish time doing so if he had it to spare. The bowdlerizations perpetrated by Mowbray Morris, the editor of *Macmillan's Magazine*, were removed in later editions.

10

A more distinguished novel, with an unhappier record of publishers' and editors' "improvements," followed. *Tess of the d'Urbervilles: A Pure Woman* had an extraordinary history. If Hardy had believed that he knew the difficulties and perils inherent in serial publication, or if he had assumed that he understood his audience on the basis of past difficulties, he was in for a dismal awakening. An introductory sketch of this nature must not linger too long on any one novel, but we must pause a moment and reëxamine Hardy's reputation at this stage. He was, by any standard, a recognized and successful novelist. His name was known to all his peers, and respected by most of them. Each new novel was read with attention, and it might even be said that Hardy, by the end of the 1880's, had become England's most distinguished writer of fiction. Macmillan wanted his next novel. *Murray's Magazine*, which had entered a prior request, awaited its receipt with high hopes. But Hardy, who had been working diligently at it from the autumn of 1888 on, submitted approximately half of the manuscript to Tillotson and Son, which ran a profitable combine called the Newspaper Fiction Bureau that sold fiction to provincial newspapers both in England and abroad. Hardy's business dealings with Tillotson's up to this point had not been extensive: three short stories between 1881 and 1887. But he did admire W. F. Tillotson personally, and the publisher's death in 1889 evoked a sincere eulogy from him. *Too Late Beloved*, as the manuscript was called (after Tess's speech to Angel Clare in Chapter 55), shocked the editors, who at once realized that a seduction and a midnight baptism were excessively controversial for their market. The contract, terminated in an atmosphere of reasonableness and good will, led to a new title as well as determined work on the rest of the story, and submission to *Murray's Magazine* in October. *Murray's* promptly rejected it because of its "improper explicitness." *Macmillan's Magazine* also found it unacceptable. The rewriting which made it acceptable for Arthur Locker and the *Graphic* is recounted, somewhat confusingly, in the *Early Life*, where Hardy does not clarify the crucial point of who exactly called for the modifications: whether Locker demanded them or Hardy "volunteered" them. But what Hardy called an "unceremonious concession to conventionality" was carried out "with cynical amusement."[13] It was "sheer drudgery," and Hardy believed that writing a different story might have been less trouble: "He resolved to get away from the supply of family fiction to magazines as soon as he conveniently could do so."

The exact nature of these alterations, the uproar which greeted the publication of *Tess*, the objections to the subtitle, the censures of Meredith, Lang, and James, and the misinterpretation of the phrase "the President of the Immortals" are all part of literary history, and need not be dwelt on here; but three matters are worth remarking. First, Hardy would have preferred to avoid serialization altogether, to bring out *Tess* as a book; but the system had trapped him (". . . there were reasons why he could not afford to do this. . ."[14]). Second, he took some pride in doing well what he thought was absurd, and what he personally knew was damaging to the artistic integrity of his book. What he scissored and trimmed, he published elsewhere as "episodic adventures of anonymous personages" or ultimately restored to the novel when it could be published as a single volume. The offending passages that he wrote in colored ink, the new passages that he wrote to cover up the scars of excisions, the work that he did to satisfy the "needs" of the *Graphic*: one might expect Hardy to be outraged, to resist. Yet Hardy recorded later that his plan for "saving" the manuscript was "till then . . . unprecedented in the annals of fiction," and, later on, "a complete success," and there is reason to believe that he derived a certain kind of grim satisfaction from outwitting the Molochs of the marketplace at their own game. Third, the reception of the novel so dismayed him that he was not only reluctant to inscribe presentation copies, but he began to think seriously about ending his career as a novelist.

The work which led to the hardening of that resolve is, in the opinion of more than one reader, Hardy's greatest achievement in prose. *Jude the Obscure* began as a series of notes in 1887, partly based on the death of a woman he had known; and the entry in the *Early Life* about a young man unable to go to Oxford who ultimately committed suicide is followed by Hardy's reflection, "There is something (in this) the world ought to be shown, and I am the one to show it to them—though I was not altogether hindered going, at least to Cambridge, and could have gone up easily at five-and-twenty."[15] Hardy had the plot fairly well outlined by 1890, and he completed the draft in March, 1895. The story, intended for publication in *Harper's Magazine*, had been promised as "a tale that could not offend the most fastidious maiden," but on April 7, 1894, Hardy asked to be allowed to withdraw from his agreement. The narrative had begun to take on a life and a direction of its own that could not be "in every respect suitable for a family magazine." Indeed, the whole history of *Tess* was to be repeated. For, although the contract was not canceled, H. M. Alden, the editor, entered into negotiations with Hardy that led to alterations of exactly the sort that had made *Tess* acceptable to the readers of the *Graphic*. Hardy's understanding of editorial dictates, tempered by a resigned but wry humor, enabled him to meet the new crisis of American purism. Alden's appreciation of the literary merits of the manuscript that he was asking Hardy to emasculate made the situation even more comic; also, perhaps, more bearable for the sensitive author.[16] Details about this arrangement are given in J. Henry Harper's *The House of Harper* (New York, 1912); editors no less than authors felt helpless before the monster of popular morality and popular taste.

Hardy's alterations, made to suit the magazine, did harm to many a reader's understanding of exactly what was going on between Jude and Sue Bridehead, or between Jude and Arabella Donn, a "mere female animal." But revising the text back to the form that Hardy had originally intended did worse harm to Hardy's sense of attachment to his story. An undated fragment (perhaps August, 1895) records the melancholy observation: ". . . I have lost energy for revising and improving the original as I meant to do."[17] Robert C. Slack's study of the textual revisions made by Hardy for subsequent editions indicates that the sorry history of patching had not completely ended. In reviewing the Osgood, McIlvaine edition of 1895 for the Macmillan edition of 1903, Hardy decided to bowdlerize the scene in which Arabella first meets Jude, that is, the scene in which a thrown pig's pizzle destroys Jude's fantasy of himself as a scholar. The second revision, made for the Macmillan text of 1912, had 206 variants: 87 stylistic, and 124 concerned with meaning in a significant way.[18] The Wessex Edition of this novel, as a consequence, is the only authoritative text one should consult; and six decades were to elapse before an edition would take account of either of the two revisions which Hardy gave *Jude the Obscure*.[19]

The novel, as publishing records show, was eminently successful, exceeding the sales of *Tess*; more than 20,000 copies were sold in less than four months. But the outcries (which Hardy believed unequaled in bitterness since the publication of Swinburne's *Poems and Ballads* in 1866) diminished Hardy's satisfaction at being read. Anonymous letters of abuse poured in. One "virtuous writer" mailed him a packet of ashes, all that was left of his "iniquitous novel." The Bishop of Wakefield claimed that he had thrown his copy of the book into the fire. Smith's Circulating Library withdrew it from the hands of its readers (at the Bishop's request). Mrs. Oliphant wrote a sharp attack in *Blackwood's* (January, 1896). In America, Jeannette Gilder published a notorious review in the *New York World* (December 8, 1895), that contained remarks on the novel's "immorality" and its "coarseness which is beyond belief."[20] Hardy very nearly lost faith in the ability of American readers to judge for themselves;

at any rate, he asked Harper's to think about the possibility of withdrawing the book from circulation.

Not long thereafter he and Mrs. Hardy visited Brussels, and the novelist paid particular attention to the battlefield of Waterloo. His ideas would later develop into thoughts of *The Dynasts*, a full-length epic-drama; but for a little while he would be absorbed with revision of *The Well-Beloved: A Sketch of a Temperament*, a rough draft of which he had written in 1891-1892. At that time he had written to Tillotson's, "There is not a word or scene in the tale which can offend the most fastidious taste; and it is equally suited for the reading of young people, and for that of persons of maturer years." But writing any novel "entirely with a view to serial publication," in Hardy's words, was a souring experience, and not only did he consider the story "short and slight," he shelved it for four years after its appearance in the *Illustrated London News* in 1892. Its revised text ran through two editions in Osgood, McIlvaine's set of the Wessex Novels, but it is remembered today primarily as Hardy's last novel, and not an outstanding one at that.

Hardy's attitude toward the novel, from the very beginning, had been a little distant. He knew that, in the modern sense, novel-writing had become a business proposition, and that in some crucial ways his temperament was not suited to the creation of "stories of modern artificial life and showing a certain smartness of treatment." It was no longer an art-form with a beginning, middle, and end; it was, rather, turning into "a spasmodic inventory of items, which has nothing to do with art."[21] Convinced of the superiority of poetry, and anxious to become a full-time poet as soon as financial circumstances would permit, he had been writing lyrics and meditative poems over a period of approximately three decades.[22]

But, on the basis of this review of his difficulties in writing for the mutual satisfaction of his audience and himself, one may draw several conclusions, first among them the likelihood that

Hardy, in his younger years at least, relished the peculiar problems associated with the serialization of fiction. In the 1870's he wrote to Leslie Stephen, "The truth is that I am willing, and indeed anxious, to give up any points which may be desirable in a story when read as a whole, for the sake of others which shall please those who read it in numbers. Perhaps I may have higher aims some day, and be a great stickler for the proper artistic balance of the completed work, but for the present circumstances lead me to wish merely to be considered a good hand at a serial."[23] He responded cheerfully to the challenge that loomed whenever a magazine began to publish installments of a work on which he was still engaged, and, indeed, there is a greater element of fun in Hardy's work during the 1870's and early 1880's than many biographers and critics appreciate. He *was* a good hand at a serial, a fact proved by the willingness, the eagerness, of editors to have him write for their publications; and he derived pleasure from knowing it.

Another, and closely related, observation is that the early direction of Hardy's development as a novelist was significantly influenced by relationships with editors. Alexander Macmillan's letter of criticism on *The Poor Man and the Lady*, dated August 10, 1868, and the first important analysis of Hardy's qualifications for the competitive market, contained the crucial sentence, "Your description of country life among working men is admirable, and, though I can only judge of it from the corresponding life in Scotland, which I knew well when young, palpably truthful."[24] *Under the Greenwood Tree*, with its skillful recreation of rustic manners and dialect, was the result; so were *A Pair of Blue Eyes* and *Far from the Madding Crowd*; and, interestingly enough, Hardy would have written still another pastoral novel to satisfy the tastes of his public if the *Spectator* reviewer had not suggested that he was beginning to sound like George Eliot. (The "woodland story" that he put aside later became *The Woodlanders*.) *The Hand of Ethelberta*—the novel which he chose to write instead—led to resentment among his readers, who apparently assumed he would write "for ever about sheepfarming." Hardy's note is appropriately dry and matter-of-fact: "He was aware of the pecuniary value of a reputation for a speciality; and . . . the acquisition of something like a regular income had become important."[25]

Nevertheless, despite all this emphasis on writing what would sell for the sake of an income that would grow, Hardy, from the very beginning, was drawn to the kind of subject matter that could only embarrass his relationships with editors. Troy's seduction of Fanny Robin; the "dangerous" relations among Eustacia, Wildeve, and Thomasin; Bishop Helmsdale's arrogance; the betrayed Tess as "a pure woman"; and Jude's description of marriage as a squashing and digesting of a person's individuality—such things might have been avoided by a writer less determined to describe human nature faithfully, by one concerned primarily with royalties. The potential dangers contained in various elements of story-telling (narrative, descriptive epithet, theme, outlook on life and society) became more rather than less conspicuous in Hardy's fictions as the century waned. Hardy was finding himself increasingly dissatisfied with the requirements of the novelist's market.

There is, in brief, an inevitability about the decision that Hardy reached late in 1896: to abandon the prose fictions which had made his reputation (or notoriety) in favor of poetry. He was older, almost sixty years of age, and somewhat wearied by controversy. His wife had been gravely disturbed by the uproar over *Jude*. He had a respectable income, and need never again depend on magazine rights for bread-money. And, as we have seen, he had always regarded novels as an inferior genre: even before he wrote his first novel, in the early 1860's, he had held the opinion that "in verse was concentrated the essence of all imaginative and emotional literature," and "never ceased to regret

17

that the author of 'the most Homeric poem in the English language—*Marmion*'—should later have declined on prose fiction."[26]

Most important, however, was the growth of his conviction that what he wanted to say could best be said in the language of poetry. For Hardy, despite the reception accorded *Jude*, had no intention of renouncing literature. The dark colorations of his later novels suggested a growing, rather than a lessening, attraction to themes of magnitude and seriousness.

On October 17, 1896, Hardy recorded the following note at Max Gate:

Poetry. Perhaps I can express more fully in verse ideas and emotions which run counter to the inert crystallized opinion—hard as a rock—which the vast body of men have vested interests in supporting. To cry out in a passionate poem that (for instance) the Supreme Mover or Movers, the Prime Force or Forces, must be either limited in power, unknowing, or cruel—which is obvious enough, and has been for centuries—will cause them merely a shake of the head; but to put it in argumentative prose will make them sneer, or foam, and set all the literary contortionists jumping upon me, a harmless agnostic, as if I were a clamorous atheist, which in their crass illiteracy they seem to think is the same thing. . . . If Galileo had said in verse that the world moved, the Inquisition might have let him alone.[27]

The memorandum offers Hardy's commentary on the difficulties of changing public opinion, and strongly implies that Hardy was unwilling to continue serving as the target of "literary contortionists." It records the adoption of a strategy, a means whereby he would outwit the self-appointed priests of the new Inquisition. The words "for instance" are misleadingly enclosed by parentheses: Hardy's greatest poem would be, in essence, his characterization of the Supreme Mover, and to it he would devote a decade of an artist's energy and writing skill. And it would be passionate, too, the most passionate and direct statement of belief that he ever converted to literature.

CHAPTER TWO

Hardy and the Universe

THE TITLE of this chapter might have been "Hardy and God," save that Hardy, as he grew older, found himself increasingly unable to speak of a ruling power as "God." Since the relationship between Hardy and whatever powers rule the universe has been of interest for almost a century, and is not always well understood even today, the following assessment is an indispensable preliminary to consideration of *The Dynasts*. I should like to discuss two syntheses of Hardy's views: the first constructed from the autobiographical statements made directly by Hardy in the two volumes put together by his wife, Florence Emily Hardy, as well as in letters that have been published in other volumes over a period of years, and the second emerging from a consideration of the novels, where such views are shaped by narrative considerations and usually are given to *personae* rather than stated directly. Only the first synthesis is trustworthy; the second, although carefully selected elements of it are of value to readers of Hardy's novels, was distorted, much to Hardy's dismay during his lifetime, and is a source of mischief to this day.

It is well to remember that Hardy's parents did not encourage unorthodox theology. Jemima Hardy, his mother, had been poor and hard-pressed in her youth. She was unable to speak objectively to her son about the painful experiences through which she had passed, and, as Hardy discovered when he explained to her his views on the meaning of existence, she did not share his opinions; she was, in fact, very much hurt by them. Hardy considered her dismay as natural but regretted it. Nevertheless, he shared with his mother at least one notion: "that a figure stands in our van with arm uplifted, to knock us back from any pleasant prospect we indulge in as probable."[1] A matriarch of ninety-one when she died in 1904, she knew that the world was not necessarily designed for man's pleasure or self-fulfillment; but her faith in a Christian God was deep-rooted and sincere.

As a grown man Hardy would attend the service at St. James in London, and this over a period of years, simply because his mother, as a young woman living in London, had attended it before he was born. Thomas Hardy, Senior, had encouraged his son to attend church services in the parish of Stinsford, Dorset, with regularity, and to pay attention to what was said. He also maintained the family tradition of supplying music for the church: conducting the choir, carol-playing, singing, in ways that were lovingly recreated by the novelist in *Under the Greenwood Tree*, with its piquant subtitle, *The Mellstock Quire*. It was in the west gallery of Stinsford Church (now removed) that Hardy's parents first saw one another; and we should not be surprised to learn, from Hardy's own account, that he would read the Morning Prayer dramatically to his cousin (representing the Clerk, and every so often saying Amen) and to his grandmother (representing the congregation). At the age of fifteen, he, together with two sons of the vicar, taught Sunday School, and for a while it almost seemed as if the remark that had so disturbed his mother —"Tommy would have to be a parson, being obviously no good for any practical pursuit"—might come true after all. He was, for example, agitated over the question of adult baptism, and on several occasions he thought of entering the Church. His intensive readings in the Greek Testament were carried on to refute two sons of the Baptist minister in Dorchester, "hard-headed Scotch youths fresh from Aberdeen University"; and although Hardy always suspected the thundering platitudes which passed for orthodoxy, he learned from these two the necessity for "plain living and high thinking."

The serious questions about the rightness of Christian doctrine raised by such works as *Essays and Reviews* (published in 1860 and read shortly after its appearance by Hardy, who thought of the volume's authors as "The Seven against Christ") were ultimately to dissuade him from matriculating at Cambridge University. If that scheme had gone through—and it could have because money would have become available for his education—he would have trained for a curacy in a country village. In 1865, in his middle twenties, he was orthodox in his attendance of Sacrament at Westminster Abbey. But his readings raised theological difficulties, and Hardy, with resignation, concluded "that he could hardly take the step with honour while holding the views which on examination he found himself to hold."[2] He was, therefore, prepared to sympathize with Leslie Stephen a decade later when called upon by the latter to witness his signature to a deed renouncing holy-orders under the act of 1870. "The deed was executed with due formality," Hardy remembered in an account written for F. W. Maitland's *Life of Leslie Stephen*. "Our conversation then turned upon theologies decayed and defunct, the origin of things, the constitution of matter, the unreality of time and kindred subjects. He told me that he had 'wasted' much time on systems of religion and metaphysics, and that the new theory of vortex rings had 'a staggering fascination' for him."[3]

The true background to Hardy's thought, as Rutland points out, may be found in the titles of books Hardy knew. We can trace through them the developing pattern of his faith in an Immanent Unrecking that drives the world to demonry. He knew intimately the Book of Job, with its emphasis on the inability of man to comprehend divine purpose. He read again and again the somber parts of the Old Testament. As an architectural student he asked Horace Moule of Queens' College, Cambridge, a budding author, whether he should continue reading Aeschylus and Sophocles in the original; and even if Moule's answer discouraged him from doing so, there is no doubt that Hardy from an early age was well acquainted with translations of the plays, and that his "bias" was strong for becoming a classical scholar. He converted one of his architectural prizes, the Sir William Tite award of three pounds, into the Bohn's translations of these playwrights. In the early 1860's, already convinced of the transiency of human life and the impossibility of achieving true happiness in this existence, he became one of the early champions of Darwin's views. On April 26, 1882, he was a spectator of Darwin's funeral in Westminster Abbey; he quoted Darwin often in later years, and in 1893 was much struck by Sir James Crichton-Browne's modification of the doctrine of survival of the fittest.

He knew Thomas Henry Huxley personally, and admired his "fearless mind." When the Rev. A. B. Grosart asked Hardy in February, 1888, to indicate how to reconcile some of the horrors of life with "the absolute goodness and non-limitation of God," so that in turn he might help the "young eager intellects" who turned to him for guidance, Hardy answered that he knew of no hypothesis that could reconcile these things, and referred him instead to a recently published life of Darwin and the works of Herbert Spencer and other agnostics; these, he said, might help Dr. Grosart "to a provisional view of the universe." And not only with Darwin, Huxley, and Spencer was he acquainted, but with Comte, whose writings on Positivism he read so carefully that some expressions "passed into his vocabulary"; with John Stuart Mill, whose three essays on religion Hardy admired and knew well, and whose treatise *On Liberty* he had practically memorized; and with Fourier, whose three abstract principles in Universal Nature—Nature, God, and Justice—he recorded in his *Trumpet Major* Notebook in the late 1870's.

As a young man, therefore, he turned to dogma-questioning books, and like any well-read man of his age, exposed himself to an impressive number of writings with an independent and even cynical tone. In the second half of the nineteenth century it was difficult for an enlightened thinker to believe that the direction of civilized endeavor was inevitably upward, or to accept uncritically the revelations and dogma of either Testament. (Hardy personally preferred to read the Old Testament, and to quote from it in his conversation and writings.) The intellectual climate of his time, rather than one or two specific books, favored the development of the mordant views of *The Dynasts.*

These comments, self-evident though they may seem, must be recorded if only as prelude to the more important statement, that Hardy's debt to Schopenhauer and Von Hartmann has been over-emphasized by scholars. Hardy, crustily honest in his acknowledgment of influences, mentioned Schopenhauer only once, in passing, in his autobiography. When Helen Garwood sent him a copy of her dissertation, Hardy denied his having been influenced by the German philosopher: his own doctrine was "a development from Schopenhauer through later philosophers."[4] In another letter he wrote, "My pages show harmony of view with Darwin, Huxley, Spencer, Comte, Hume, Mill, and others, all of whom I used to read more than Schopenhauer."[5] We have no direct evidence that Hardy read very much (or any) of R. B. Haldane and J. Kemp's translation of *The World as Will and Idea,* which Trübner published in London in 1883. We do know, however, that Hardy purchased, around 1890, a copy of Mrs. Karl Hillebrand's translation of *On the Four-Fold Root of the Principle of Sufficient Reason,* published by George Bell and Sons in London in 1889; that he cut its leaves; and that he marked passages of particular interest to himself. It has been suggested that Hardy derived from this volume his concept of Will as "effort exercised in an . . . unconscious manner"; his distinction between Will and Free-Will; and his cause for "final Hope" in the supposition that conscious life is itself a manifestation of will.[6]

This is more reasonably argued than the views put forward in either Helen Garwood's study or Ernest Brennecke, Jr.'s *Thomas Hardy's Universe: A Study of a Poet's Mind* (London, 1924), the publication of which so exercised Hardy in his final years. Brennecke is given to such generalizations as the following: "It is quite safe to add that if Hardy had not in his later years come in contact with the work of Schopenhauer, *The Dynasts* could never have assumed its present form, largely determined by the characteristic expressions that run through its 'Overworld' scenes" (pp. 144-145). Few statements are less safe. But there exist difficulties preventing us from attributing so much influence to *any* single book: the fact that Mill also had written about the possibility of the existence of unconscious Mind, or Will[7]; the fact that Schopenhauer's doctrine is not meliorist in the same sense as the final statement of *The Dynasts*[8]; and the fact that Hardy himself seems to be talking about later commentators on Schopenhauer —Von Hartmann, for one—rather than Schopenhauer himself.

Nevertheless, it is easier to disentangle the views of Schopenhauer from those of Von Hartmann than it is to measure the influence of either on Hardy's mature philosophy. Von Hartmann's book, *Philosophy of the Unconscious*, was first translated into English in 1884, and, as at least one scholar believes, served as Hardy's sourcebook for "a workable theory of the great problem of the origin of evil."[9] Von Hartmann modified Schopenhauer; changed the word "Will" to the word "Unconscious"; argued that consciousness, as well as impulses from the Unconscious, might be a ground for action; and added a note of hope, or meliorism, which Hardy echoed in his concluding Chorus: "Consciousness the Will informing, till it fashion all things fair!"

But exactly the same objections apply to such a strong case for Von Hartmann's influence. There is the second of Mill's *Essays on Religion*, with its critical formulation of how conscious Mind may be produced by unconscious processes, and with its prior date of at least fourteen years. There is Hardy's censure of Von Hartmann's "supercilious regard of hope," which the poet contrasted with his own "forlorn" but determined hope.[10] And how "iffy" such postulations are! The argument that Hardy discovered a developing consciousness in the Unconscious because Von Hartmann suggested the idea to him, or that Hardy so completely assimilated Von Hartmann's hypothesis that "he even thought he had originated it,"[11] is debatable. We cannot say for a certainty which speeches of the Spirits in *The Dynasts* represent Hardy's

24

personal doctrine; many of them do, but not all. It seems unlikely, too, that the phrase "clock-like laws," recorded in the Fore Scene, or the comment that the Immanent Will is "possessed" and does not judge, contains some significant condemnation of scientific determinism. Hardy's commitment was to a determinism which had scientific sanction in the writings of his day, and Hardy had no need to become a schoolboy late in the 1880's.

On this matter—a crucial one for the appreciation of much of the discussion which follows—Hardy remains the best witness, and it is astonishing that his words are so often ignored by writers anxious to explain or popularize his writings. Hardy believed that the Immanent Will could be traced to a period of time far earlier than Schopenhauer's discussions. In a famous colloquy with a reviewer for the *Times*, Hardy declared that the philosophy of *The Dynasts*, "under various titles and phrases, is almost as old as civilization." "Its fundamental principle, under the name of Predestination," he went on, "was preached by St. Paul. . . . It has run through the history of the Christian Church ever since. St. Augustine held it vaguely. Calvin held it fiercely, and, if our English Church and its Nonconformist contemporaries have almost abandoned it to our men of science (among whom determinism is a commonplace), it was formerly taught by Evangelical divines of the finest character and conduct."[12] Hardy knew that the past sanctioned his view of the universe. On June 2, 1907, writing to Edward Wright, he stated that the concept of an Unconscious Will was "what the thinking world had gradually come to adopt," himself included[13]; but he never implied that the adoption could be dated as late as the 1880's. To Alfred Noyes, on December 19, 1920, he wrote that his concept of the Cause of Things was "that of a great many ordinary thinkers."[14]

For that matter, these attempts to emphasize the influence of Schopenhauer and Von Hartmann on Hardy have seriously distorted Hardy's achievement as a poet and dramatist. For Hardy never thought of himself as a philosopher; he troubled himself very little about theories; to him only pure mathematics illustrated "perfect reason." Although he read a great many philosophers, he subscribed wholly to none because their "contradictions and futilities" depressed him. On December 31, 1901, he wrote a memorandum to himself, ". . . Let every man make a philosophy for himself out of his own experience. He will not be able to escape using terms and phraseology from earlier philosophers, but let him avoid adopting their theories if he values his own mental life. Let him remember the fate of Coleridge, and save years af labour by working out his own views as given him by his surroundings." To write *The Dynasts*, some philosophy seemed called for; but his objective was to create poetry, not to define the mind of the age, or even to be true. In his Preface he made his intention unmistakable: the doctrines of the Spirits were "but tentative," and were "advanced with little eye to a systematized philosophy warranted to lift 'the burthen of the mystery' of this unintelligible world." The chief thing Hardy hoped for them was that "they and their utterances" might have "dramatic plausibility enough to procure for them, in the words of Coleridge, 'that willing suspension of disbelief for the moment which constitutes poetic faith.'" If there existed discrepancies, if the doctrine seemed new, if it did not seem new, he did not care. Hardy's intention was to create an imaginative work; his plea was that *The Dynasts* would be read and judged as such.

What, then, are Hardy's views on the nature of the universe and of man's relationship to it? He regarded the universe as an enormously complicated and imperfect machine, "a world of defect." Responding to German writers and artists who wished to commemorate the seventieth anniversary of Nietzsche's birth, Hardy wrote that Nietzsche's faith in the powers of man was misplaced: ". . . to do good with an ill-working instrument requires endless adjustments and compromises."

Such compromises are tragic to the thinking man: "The widened view of nowadays perceives that the world weeps and mourns all round."[15] The world was not made to be a "comfort-able place" for man. Pain should not be excused by specious argument, as in Maeterlinck's *Apology for Nature*. We can love our neighbor as ourselves only if we understand that pain has always been part of the scheme of things, and if we feel the pain of others as keenly as if it affects us directly. All living things suffer (Hardy's intense compassion for dumb animals abused by war or careless owners should not be forgotten), and the line between life and death is narrow at best.

Hardy called the ruling principle Law or Necessity rather than God, and he suggested that limitations prevented this Law from doing all that It desired to do for Its creature, Man. The ineffectualness of the One Principle "striving for our good, but unable to achieve it except occasionally"[16] was a favorite theme in Hardy's mind. In some of his earliest jottings for *The Dynasts*, Hardy thought of writing a poem on the subject of a First Cause, "omniscient, not omnipotent—limitations, difficulties, etc., from being only able to work by Law (His only failing is lack of fore-sight)."[17] And late in his life, as if reluctant to have even this kind of personal doctrine mistaken for a faith in a traditional or Christian God, Hardy wrote that the First Cause might very well be a convenient way of talking about "a thousand unconscious causes—lumped together in poetry as one Cause, or God. . . ."[18]

But whatever It was, It lacked malevolence. Hardy rejected many of his critics' views as basely Philistine whenever they accused him of personally believing in a vengeful "President of the Immortals." He had used the phrase in its classical sense, borrowing it from a translation of *Prometheus Bound* prepared by Theodore A. Buckley and published in 1849, for the conclusion of *Tess of the d'Urbervilles*. But he was not a "primitive believer" in any "man-shaped tribal god," and, reacting against misinterpretations of the philosophy contained in the concluding part of *The Dynasts*, he insisted that he had merely surmised "an indifferent and unconscious force at the back of things 'that neither good nor evil knows.' "[19] In a spirited exchange of letters with Alfred Noyes, conducted in December, 1920, Hardy stressed again "the vast difference between the expression of fancy and the expression of belief." He had never called the Power behind the Universe "an imbecile jester"; rather, it was *un*moral, "loveless and hateless." He concluded with the melancholy observation that "the Scheme of Things is, indeed, incomprehensible; and there I suppose we must leave it—perhaps for the best. Knowledge might be terrible."

Yet for exactly such knowledge he had searched, all his life. He had never found God "as an external personality . . . the only true meaning of the word."[20] He could entertain suspicions: for example, that Nature might have exceeded her "mission" in allowing invertebrates to develop into vertebrates. He could be angry at cheap substitutes for faith, as his note for August 15, 1897, indicates: "It is so easy nowadays to call any force above or under the sky by the name of 'God'—and so pass as orthodox cheaply, and fill the pocket!" He could convince himself that "the days of creeds are as dead and done with as days of Pterodactyls,"[21] and that liturgical reform was essential if the churches were to avoid becoming the centers of solely antiquarian interest. Beneath all his flashes of anger at obtuseness, bigotry, and insincerity, there ran an even more deep and powerful undercurrent of feeling, a hard-won, personal emotion that may not be dismissed as mere crankiness.

He thought of himself as a man interested in the principle of non-rationality that lay "at the indifference point between rationality and irrationality," and for that reason he deliberately chose "non-rationalistic subjects." Thus, he could refuse Joseph McCabe's proposal to include him in a biographical dictionary of twentieth-century rationalists on the grounds that "no man is a rationalist, and . . . human actions are not ruled by reason at all in the last resort."[22]

He was, more than anything else, a man determined to face

the truth, and if others chose to call him a Pessimist, he would answer that "it is the only view of life in which you can never be disappointed." This doctrine, recorded in these words on January 1, 1902, had been shaped long before, by the 1860's, and it underwent no major change for the rest of his life. He believed, along with Heine, that the soul had her eternal rights. "And what is to-day, in allusions to the present author's pages, alleged to be 'pessimism' is, in truth, only such 'questionings' in the exploration of reality, and is the first step towards the soul's betterment, and the body's also."[23] His was the doctrine of the Gospels, of much of the Greek drama; and he never stated it more succinctly than in the second of his three poems, "In Tenebris" (1895-96), where the following line appears:

Who holds that if way to the Better there be, it exacts a full look at the Worst.

It is true that Hardy's dark reading of the meaning of the universe, and his denial of any anthropomorphic god, were balanced to some degree by his trust that a better consummation was possible. The condition of "mindlessness" might be coming to an end, as he wrote in one of his final poems, "A Philosophical Fantasy" (published in the *Fortnightly Review* in January, 1927), and he considered that possibility "a ray of hope." He consoled himself by saying at irregular intervals that the existence of a God was so vast an inquiry that its very vastness made the whole question unimportant. Convinced by experience that "nothing bears out in practice what it promises incipiently," he shied away from glib philosophy quite as much as from orthodox theology; a theory could not explain everything. Yet, at the same time, he denied the relativistic doctrine of pragmatism. After quoting William James's statement that "Truth is what will work," he entered in his notebook, "A worse corruption of language was never perpetrated."

The overwhelming impression most readers have of Thomas

Hardy's universe is that the evolutionary meliorism of which Hardy said he was a spokesman seems less conspicuous than his conviction, everywhere implicit, that 'this planet does not supply the materials for happiness to higher existences. Other planets may, though one can hardly see how."[24] It may be useful to list the reasons why his philosophy was proudly Pessimistic in the very sense he gave that word.

As the discussion may have already made clear, his independent readings raised important issues that formal creeds could not satisfactorily answer. Hardy's friendship for somebody he highly respected—Horace M. Moule—led him, at the age of twenty, to a close study of Newman's *Apologia*; he wished to be "convinced"; but the lack of a first link to Newman's "excellent chain of reasoning" counted for more than charming style or human logic; and down he came headlong.[25] It was like that all his life: he wanted to believe, and could not at the crucial moment because of a nagging sense that something more was wanting. In 1883 he swore that he would be his own judge, no matter what others thought. "In future I am not going to praise things because the accumulated remarks of ages say they are great and good, if those accumulated remarks are not based on observation. And I am not going to condemn things because a pile of accepted views raked together from tradition, and acquired by instillation, say antecedently that they are bad."[26] It is not just to say that Hardy rejected Christianity without due misgivings; or that he became a Pessimist without considering the alternatives. His library at Max Gate, before a large part of it was scattered by auction sales, was carefully annotated and underlined, and many of the volumes were theological or metaphysical.

He was also reacting against the strict church indoctrination of his youth. His novels and poems, filled as they are with echoes of the Burial Service, of the Psalms, of hymns and responses, bear witness that the influence of those early years never disappeared from his thinking. He was, indeed, "churchy," as he himself wrote, "not in an intellectual sense, but in so far as instincts and emotions ruled."[27] But his faith was in good works, in the finding of means to ease "mortals' progress through a world not worthy of them," in "the religion of emotional morality and altruism" that countless religions, including Christianity, taught. The autobiography is understandably reticent on this point because Hardy's decision not to become a parson must have pained his mother; but the evidence suggests that the decision to renounce a career within the Church was made in August, 1865, in London, while he was working as an apprentice to the architect Arthur Blomfield.

A third explanation of Hardy's unsentimental concept of the universe is physical. The illnesses that Hardy suffered, particularly the one that incapacitated him during the writing of *A Laodicean*, made him acutely, even morbidly, sensitive to the frailties of flesh. There were days when he actually did not think he would live till evening. Once, after he had hurt his tooth and was looking in the mirror, he became conscious of "the humiliating sorriness" of his "earthly tabernacle." He added, "Why should a man's mind have been thrown into such close, sad, sensational, inexplicable relations with such a precarious object as his own body!"[28] At unexpected moments he experienced horror at the thought of vast crowds of people huddled together, and all his life he had an extreme distaste against being touched in any way. These attacks of nerves were, of course, sometimes founded on genuine physical disorders; but psychologically, too, they invite closer examination as a contributory factor to the writing of several celebrated passages in his literary creations.

Again, we must not forget Hardy's problem with reviewers. This is not a trivial matter. Hardy was frequently misunderstood, too often harshly judged by critics out to make a reputation (women reviewers in America, he believed, were especially offensive), and occasionally praised for the wrong reasons. Stupid reviews would not have mattered save for two reasons: they could affect a writer's sales, and Hardy read them carefully. He read one of his first hostile reviews (the *Spectator's* slating of *Desperate Remedies* in 1871) while sitting on a stile near Bockhampton. "The bitterness of that moment was never forgotten," he told his wife several decades later; "at the time he wished that he were dead."[29] A review of *Tess* in the *Quarterly* was instrumental in his decision, not very long thereafter, to abandon prose narratives as a means of earning a living: "Well, if this sort of thing continues no more novel-writing for me. A man must be a fool to deliberately stand up to be shot at."[30] The responses to *Jude* soured him so that he wrote shortly after his birthday, "Every man's birthday is a first of April for him; and he who lives to be fifty and won't own it is a rogue or a fool, hypocrite or simpleton."[31] Late in his life, when World War I seemed to be a fixed part of the English scene, never to leave, he jotted down some tart comments on reviewing: "Apart from a few brilliant exceptions, poetry is not at bottom criticized as such, that is, as a particular man's artistic interpretation of life, but with a secret eye on its theological and political propriety." It is striking, and symptomatic, that he followed this judgment of contemporary criticism with a restatement of his views on pessimism.[32] Charles Morgan, who as Manager for the Oxford University Dramatic Society was the official welcomer to Hardy, up from Max Gate to see a special performance of *The Dynasts* in 1920, was particularly impressed by the somber cast of Hardy's comments on his reviewers. Hardy's bitterness surprised Morgan, and seemed unjustified to him; but the fact that Hardy ventured on the subject without provocation from Morgan, and spoke with strong feeling, "sadly rather than querulously," means that the matter was never far from his mind. Hardy's relations to his reviewers were, on the whole, less unfortunate than he believed. However, his acute sensitivity to what they said never hardened over, and rendered him vulnerable to almost any sneer from any source, however unenlightened or unworthy of his attention.

32

Also, many of the most important poems published during the second half of the nineteenth century had a pessimistic hue. F. A. Aulard's three-volume translation into French (Paris, 1880) of Count Giacomo Leopardi's poems was in his library. Edward FitzGerald's version of *The Rubáiyát of Omar Khayyám* had achieved notoriety, and success, by the 1880's; FitzGerald noted that the lyrics, whether "Grave or Gay," were "more apt to move Sorrow than Anger toward the old Tent-maker, who, after vainly endeavoring to unshackle his steps from Destiny, and to catch some authentic glimpse of *Tomorrow*, fell back upon *Today* (which has outlasted so many Tomorrows!) as the only Ground he got to stand upon, however momentarily slipping from under his Feet." And, without pressing the resemblance between Hardy and any specific Victorian poet, we may note that Swinburne, whose work Hardy admired, treated the Christian church as a malignant influence; that Arnold, whom Hardy read attentively, felt frustrated between two worlds, one dead, the other powerless to be born; that Arthur Hugh Clough, whom Arnold elegized in "Thyrsis," had been appalled by the direction of Victorian life; that the Pre-Raphaelites were customarily gloomy in their celebrations of frustrated love; that George Meredith—a judiciously sympathetic reader of Hardy's first attempt at a novel, *The Poor Man and the Lady*—attempted, like Hardy, to reconcile the findings of modern science with traditional theology, and did so more successfully than Hardy partly because he reinterpreted the concept of "spirit" in a social rather than a Christian sense; that Tennyson's view of the new science was suspicious when not actually hostile; and that the admirers of Baudelaire and Verlaine—Lionel Johnson, Ernest Dowson, Oscar Wilde, John Davidson, Francis Thompson—formed a singularly ill-starred group. Among Hardy's contemporaries, too, must be listed James Thomson, the author of perhaps the most relentlessly pessimistic poem in all English literature. *The City of Dreadful Night*, first published in the *National Reformer* in March-May,

1874, adopted its motto from Leopardi: "In thee, O Death, our naked nature finds repose; not joyful, but safe from the old sadness." (Late in his life Thomson prepared some distinguished translations of Leopardi.) It describes a "fell" Destiny, a Limbo within which the inhabitants of the desert must dwell, "shut out alike from heaven and earth and hell." For this world Thomson could imagine "no purpose, heart or mind or will." The Heavens, despite their stars, are "sightless." Any God who—when He might refrain—would form such creatures, doomed to their despair and knowledge of the purposelessness of existence, disgraced Himself; but Thomson, like Hardy, did not believe in a malevolent deity, and his point of view is most directly expressed by the "great sad voice deep and full" of the poem's fourteenth section.

> This little life is all we must endure,
> The grave's most holy peace is ever sure,
>   We fall asleep and never wake again;
> Nothing is of us but the moldering flesh,
> Whose elements dissolve and merge afresh
>   In earth, air, water, plants, and other men. . . .
>
> All substance lives and struggles evermore
> Through countless shapes continually at war,
>   By countless interactions interknit;
> If one is born a certain day on earth,
> All times and forces tended to that birth,
>   Not all the world could change or hinder it.
>
> I find no hint throughout the Universe
> Of good or ill, of blessing or of curse;
>   I find alone Necessity Supreme. . . .

These views—mechanistic, materialistic, and grimly necessitarian —were in large measure Hardy's; and he had come to a full realization of them before he was forty years of age, for the various reasons listed above. He was not, in all fairness, holding to idiosyncratic views, nor was his Pessimism unshared. The statement which Hardy made many times over to the effect that his "sober opinion" of the Cause of Things had been defined in scores of places was entirely justified. He drew controversy to himself primarily because—in scattered passages, phrases, or incidents—he sought to convey these ideas through the medium of the novel, which, like any product intended for mass circulation, cannot afford to offend the cherished, if unexamined, prejudices of the compact majority.

Now it is dangerous to ascribe to Hardy the opinions of his fictional characters, even if one is so taken by their convincingness that these personages seem as real as historical figures. The attempt has been made, several times, to trace through the novels changes in Hardy's concept of just what or who is responsible for man's unfortunate condition. (That his condition *is* unfortunate, Hardy believed, of course, from the very beginning.) A few works are usually selected as indicative of major shifts of emphasis. *Far from the Madding Crowd*, for example, contains Henery Fray's lament, "Your lot is your lot, and Scripture is nothing," and the opinion that Destiny cheats a man out of his "recompense" for doing good. *The Return of the Native* notes the "long line of disillusive centuries" which has replaced the Greek zest for existence with a view of life "as a thing to be put up with"; Hardy concludes, "What the Greeks only suspected we know well; what their Aeschylus imagined our nursery children feel" (Book III, Chapter 1). The strongest statement of what causes misery is made by Eustacia, at the climax of her tragic life, when she moans about her helplessness before superior forces: "O, the cruelty of putting me into this ill-conceived world! I was capable of much; but I have been injured and blighted and crushed by things beyond my control! O, how hard it is of Heaven to devise such tortures for me, who have done no harm to Heaven at all!" To her, man is the unwilling instrument of a diabolical Prince of the World.

35

The Mayor of Casterbridge, however, emphasizes the dictum of the German romanticist Novalis, "Character is Fate," and suggests that Michael Henchard, the unhappy hero, loses "all that can make life interesting, or even tolerable . . . either by his fault or by his misfortune." Happiness is "but the occasional episode in a general drama of pain," but man is more responsible than he admits for the direction established by his "brief transit through a sorry world."

The Woodlanders indicates something new: society, and the institutions which it supports, may be the critical determinants of an individual's life. A desire to climb the social ladder may lead to a marriage that mocks God's name: did God, after all, really join together Grace Melbury and Edred Fitzpiers? or did her father push her into it for the furtherance of his own schemes?

Tess is even more openly didactic, and as a book its rebellion becomes overtly passionate. "God's not in his heaven: all's wrong with the world!"[33] Wordsworth's paean,

> Not in utter nakedness
> But trailing clouds of glory do we come,

impresses Tess as "ghastly satire," and Hardy adds, "To her and her like, birth itself was an ordeal of degrading personal compulsion, whose gratuitousness nothing in the result seemed to justify, and at best could only palliate."[34]

For *Jude*, a novel aflame with criticism of the age, it did not avail Hardy, in his original Preface, to say: "For a novel addressed by a man to men and women of full age; which attempts to deal unaffectedly with the fret and fever, derision and disaster, that may press in the wake of the strongest passion known to humanity; to tell, without a mincing of words, of a deadly war waged between flesh and the spirit; and to point the tragedy of unfulfilled aims, I am not aware that there is anything in the handling to which exception can be taken."[35] Too much within the story amounted to sociological condemnation for some readers to accept the book objectively. Jude's cry to the Christminster crowd on Remembrance Day—"I may do some good before I am dead—be a sort of success as a frightful example of what not to do; and so illustrate a moral story"—offended many who believed that marriage vows, no matter how ill-matched the married couple, must be treated as sacred. The story of Jude Fawley, the South Wessex villager, and Sue Bridehead, his cousin, became an indictment of the world which demanded conformity from such proud, unhappy people. "I was, perhaps, after all, a paltry victim to the spirit of mental and social restlessness that makes so many unhappy in these days!" Jude continued. ". . . And what I appear, a sick and poor man, is not the worst of me. I am in a chaos of principles—groping in the dark—acting by instinct and not after example. . . . I perceive there is something wrong somewhere in our social formulas: what it is can only be discovered by men or women with greater insight than mine,—if, indeed, they ever discover it—at least in our time. 'For who knoweth what is good for man in this life?—and who can tell a man what shall be after him under the sun?'" Society had become a "chaos of principles."

But Hardy's personal opinions are not necessarily reflected by these changing assignations of responsibility for man's unhappiness. Nobody was more determined to avoid blame for what fictional characters believed than their creator, and it is odd that Hardy's admirers no less than his detractors should seek to establish so close a correlation. For example, he denied that *Jude* was a manifesto on the marriage question; said so in the novel; repeated it in letters to friends; and still was not believed. Primarily concerned with writing the story of a student's relationship to a University, and with that young man's special marriage situations, Hardy assured his friends that no novel was less autobiographical; and wrote, late in life, that a hundred lines of his poetry were more truly autobiographical than all his novels. To him there was a "vast difference between the expression of fancy and the expression of belief," as he wrote to Alfred Noyes on December 19, 1920, in a letter remarkable for the care with which he disavowed the views contained in more than half a dozen poems. There seems no valid reason why we should disbelieve Hardy when he states that his poems are "dramatic or personative in conception; and this even where they are not obviously so."[36] In addition, there exists no pressing need to compress his "unadjusted impressions," recorded over a period of decades, into a single mood or a single philosophy of life. A matter that might more meaningfully reveal something of Hardy's attitude toward life is the unexpected juxtaposition of serious and lightly humorous poems: but even here we must walk warily, because Hardy found arranging his poems in a meaningful sequence a difficult and finally an impossible task. "I must trust for right note-catching to those finely-touched spirits," he wrote, "who can divine without half a whisper, whose intuitiveness is proof against all the accidents of inconsequence. In respect of the less alert, however, should any one's train of thought be thrown out of gear by a consecutive piping of vocal reeds in jarring tonics, without a semiquaver's rest between, and be led thereby to miss the writer's aim and meaning in one of two contiguous compositions, I shall deeply regret it."[37]

One crucial value, however, resides in the discussion of fictional attitudes, and this quite apart from the fact that such discussion can clarify our understanding of the intention as well as the achievement of works of art. We can see that Hardy's perception of the limitations of a thoroughgoing deterministic doctrine is not fixed at the intellectual level of Eustacia Vye. Other explanations of man's unhappiness are possible: man's perversity; the institutions of society; or possibly even what Hardy called "Hap."

I have spoken at such length about what led to Hardy's pessimism, and about the dangers of identifying Hardy's views with those of any of his fictional characters, because the Immanent Will in *The Dynasts*, it seems to me, is best understood as a meta-

phor for the meaning of existence, and not as some kind of il-
luminated anatomy in which Hardy literally believed. It is appreciated, in other words, as a creation of an artist.

Before we consider the artistic merits of this, Hardy's longest
and greatest poem, a brief review of the circumstances of composition will be useful.

CHAPTER THREE

The Background of *The Dynasts*

IT IS NOT EASY to say when or how Hardy first conceived the idea of writing a full-length epic-drama about the Napoleonic epoch between 1805 and 1815. In later years he indicated that he himself had forgotten. On March 13, 1874, he wrote in the first of his three unpublished notebooks, "Let Europe be the stage and have scenes continually shifting." A long time afterwards, in puzzlement, he added the parenthetical question, "Can this refer to any conception of *The Dynasts*?"[1] In 1875 he also recorded a note about the possibility of writing "A Ballad of the Hundred Days," another of Moscow, and several of earlier campaigns, "forming altogether an Iliad of Europe from 1789 to 1815."[2] For his autobiography he labeled it his "earliest note."

The possibility of such a work had always been with him; from his childhood he had been close to people who could remember those remarkable years. His grandmother had told him stories about Boney. He was related, however distantly, to Captain Hardy of *H.M.S. Victory*, and although proof of the exact degree of relationship came into his hands when he was an old man, he had always believed that the relationship existed. His grandfather had been a volunteer in the patriotic mustering of English folk against the Corsican tyrant. During Hardy's boyhood people spoke with pride of their vivid memories of the "Bang-up-Locals" who had defended the English coast.[3] And it was his father, most probably, who purchased and kept available in the home the two volumes of C. H. Gifford's *History of the Wars Occasioned by the French Revolution, 1792-1816* (London, 1817).

Odds and ends testified mutely to the stay of George III at Weymouth between 1798 and 1805: for example, the King's bathing machine, or the sockets for the standards bearing the red cord which had divided the royal dancers from the people of the town at Gloucester Lodge.

The work necessary "to keep base life afoot" prevented him from writing his *Iliad* for more than two decades. Nevertheless, the process of acquiring the raw materials of such a work continued intermittently while he was writing novels on totally unrelated themes. Even though he was to change the beginning year of his chronicle from the outbreak of the French Revolution to Napoleon's second coronation at Milan, he saw, from the beginning, that the logical place to end the story would be Waterloo. It was impossible for him to forget the connections between some of his distinguished contemporaries and the magnetic figure of Napoleon. As a young man, he was thrilled by the opportunity to hear Palmerston, the former War Secretary, a man who had contributed to the direction of the war against Napoleon, speak in the House of Commons shortly before his death. He attended the funeral of young Louis Napoleon at Chislehurst in 1879, and was much impressed by Prince Napoleon's profile: "complexion dark, sallow, even sinister: a round projecting chin: countenance altogether extraordinarily remindful of Boney."[4] The sight proved useful when, for *The Dynasts*, Hardy had to imagine the Emperor's appearance. He went out of his way to talk to the pensioners at Chelsea Hospital who had fought in the Peninsula as well as at Waterloo: going there in 1870; again in 1875, on the sixtieth anniversary of the battle of Waterloo, to talk to "a delightful old campaigner" named John Bentley; still again, in 1876 on Waterloo Day, to relive the battle "over glasses of grog" with "the dwindling number of pensioners who had taken part in it"; and in 1878, to reminisce with "a palsied pensioner" almost in his ninth decade, about "that terrible winter march to Coruña" which he had shared with Sir John Moore ("It was extraordinary to talk and shake hands" with him, Hardy remembered). Meeting descendants of those who had participated in eventful days was enough to start echoes moving in his mind, as, for example, in

41

1883, when he met an old man related to one of the keepers of Rainbarrows' Beacon, whose duty had been to keep watch on the sea from which a French invasion force might come.

There were also his visits to Waterloo, the first in 1876, when he investigated the probable site of the fabled ball given by the Duchess of Richmond the evening before the fateful clash of arms. The results of his search were unsatisfactory. Twenty years later, in 1896, he returned to the same hotel in Brussels, and again visited the field: "Walked alone from the English line along the Charleroi Road to 'La Belle Alliance.' Struck with the *nearness* of the French and English lines to each other."[5] He was, by this time, conducting formal research, and if for a second time the scene of the ball remained undiscoverable, he knew how he wanted to dramatize the action: he had named his work "Europe in Throes," and he conceived of it as having three parts, each with five acts.[6]

To these personal associations of what he had seen, and the people he knew and talked to, must be added his extensive readings. He used Gifford's *History* for the writing of *The Trumpet-Major*, which dealt in large measure with the pressures exerted by the Napoleonic Wars on young Englishmen of military age, and was to use it again. He read as many contemporary newspapers as he could; transcribed the "Address to all Ranks and Descriptions of Englishmen" from an original copy in a museum; studied the Army Regulations for 1801; borrowed information from *The Adventures and Recollections of Colonel Landmann* (London, 1852); looked over the plates of Rowlandson and Ackermann; and acquired a respectable, if oddly assorted, quantity of information about the Services. For *The Dynasts*, he returned to the notebook he had kept for his earlier novel about this period, and he expanded his information in as many ways as possible.[7] William R. Rutland, who speaks of *The Dynasts* as "the greatest imaginative representation of the Napoleonic epoch in the literature of Western Europe," has written a useful study of how Hardy used historical sources for I, V (primarily about Trafalgar). Hardy had approximately one hundred volumes, judiciously selected for his purposes, at Max Gate, and he probably consulted some of the volumes dealing with Napoleon's era in the library of A. M. Broadley, his neighbor.[8] Hardy found particularly useful A. Thiers' *Histoire du Consulat et de l'Empire* (available to him both in French and English editions); J. Capefigue's *L'Europe pendant le Consulat et l'Empire de Napoléon Ier* (Paris, 1840); P. Coquelle's *Napoléon et l'Angleterre, 1803-1813* (Paris, 1904); W. F. P. Napier's *History of the War in the Peninsula* (London, 1892); and, as Rutland demonstrates in his analysis of the Trafalgar scenes, Edward Pelham Brenton's *The Naval History of Great Britain, 1783-1822* (London, 1823).

From the beginning, Hardy had no intention of simply describing a decade of history. His early jotting to the effect that the ballad might be a suitable form, and his citation of the *Iliad* as a classical precedent, indicated that he associated the epic with the ballad in some way. The epic, to be sure, has venerable roots in English literary history, and more will soon be said about the relationships between Hardy's work and Milton's *Paradise Lost*. But Hardy had to make a massive effort—to invent a genre, in fact—to accommodate these large movements of armies and governments. Only a partial explanation of his intense interest may be found in either the involvement of members of his family or the availability of printed sources. After all, if his primary intention was to find an outlet for his views of the nature and function of Immanent Will, other themes from the past, from the lives of his Wessex farmers and townspeople, were readily available. They were well known to him, more manageable. A stronger motivation lay in the fact that he was convinced the epical qualities of the Napoleonic struggle had hitherto been minimized or ignored.

Hardy came gradually to a sense of the true moral inherent in his subject-matter: all dynasties are self-defeating if the rulers of Europe are concerned only with maintaining their dynasties rather than benefiting their peoples.[9] The Spirit of the Pities makes clear the lesson to be drawn from Albuera, "the sanguinary scene of the most murderous struggle of the whole war" in Spain:

> On earth below
> Are men—unnatured and mechanic-drawn—
> Mixt nationalities in row and row,
>   Wheeling them to and fro
> In moves dissociate from their souls' demand,
> For dynasts' ends that few even understand. (II, VI, iv)

It is the same lesson to be learned from every war provoked into being by Napoleon's schemes. The desires of the peoples of Europe to live in peace were continually frustrated by the reigning sovereigns. Nevertheless, the record of Hardy's annotations on what he planned to do shows that not until relatively late did the emphasis fall upon the adventurings of other kings as well as Napoleon. The Corsican prospered as one of many dynasts; he, like other kings, fed in predatory fashion on the weaknesses of lieutenants, friends, and enemies. As Hardy finally saw, the culpability was international. The greed for power raged unabated after the frightful casualties of the Grand Army on the retreat from Moscow, the holocaust of the Bridge of the Beresina; these things were but incidents in the convulsive agonies of the "Christ of War"; and every nation smirked in satisfaction to see the overthrow of the Emperor.

Hardy at first thought of Napoleon as an interesting figure in a conventional narrative. In 1868 he outlined a poem on the Battle of the Nile, "as material for poetry of some sort," but never finished it because work on *The Poor Man and the Lady* absorbed his energies, and because novel-writing, as we have seen, distracted him from any long poem—and from the plays in blank verse he had briefly thought of writing—for some thirty years.

Within a few years, however, he had moved from this vaguely romantic treatment of a single campaign to a larger view of all the Napoleonic Wars. By June, 1877, his concept of a ballad-sequence had become transformed to a "grand drama" which would demand a huge cast of characters. He was still not sure how to focus his knowledge: "It might be called 'Napoleon,' " he wrote, "or 'Josephine,' or by some other person's name."[10] He did know, at any rate, that his work would not resemble a Shakespearean history-play. His view of Napoleon's career was searching for a mode or genre that would not arouse familiar, and misleading, associations in the unwary reader who might be accustomed by flights of rhetoric to search for heroic stances.

The next important step was to recognize the possibility of having all Humanity as his *dramatis personae*. Hardy's old notes, copied in 1922, bear no date; but I believe, on the basis of internal evidence, that he first recorded them somewhere around 1880. At the Lord Mayor's Show on Ludgate Hill in 1879, Hardy and his wife were impressed by the impossibility of identifying individuals in the surging crowd. "As the crowd grows denser," Hardy commented, "it loses its character of an aggregate of countless units, and becomes an organic whole, a molluscous black creature having nothing in common with humanity, that takes the shape of the streets along which it has lain itself, and throws out horrid excrescences and limbs into neighboring alleys; a creature whose voice exudes from its scaly coat, and who has an eye in every pore of its body." This passage resembles another, made within a few months, written to explain his insomnia: an eerie feeling "sometimes haunted him, a horror at lying down in close proximity to 'a monster whose body had four million heads and eight million eyes.' " Humanity had become "a collective personality" in this sense, and when Hardy, adapting his vision to literary terms, imagined such a personality within a drama about Napoleon's age, he saw it battling for an unknown cause. "Title 'self-slaughter'; 'divided against ourselves.' "[11] In March, 1886, he visualized the human race "as one great network or tissue which quivers in every part when one point is shaken, like a spider's web if touched. Abstract realisms to be in the form of Spirits, Spectral figures, etc." With the introduction of celestial machinery, he had gone a long way toward defining the form of his epic-drama.

If, therefore, these notes are datable to approximately 1880, another observation becomes pertinent: Hardy, at an early stage, knew what *tone* he wanted to adopt. The first poem that he wanted to write would illustrate "the difference between what things are and what they ought to be. (Stated as by a god to the gods—*i.e.* as God's story.)" He saw himself as ironical, detached, genially amused at the sight of an army fighting "as somnambulists—not knowing what it is for." He imagined, too, the pathos inherent in the compulsion that could operate, as spectral force, in a man such as Napoleon.[12]

The ballad form, in brief, could not accommodate his widening views of what a "Great Modern Drama" should treat.[13] Torn between his admiration of traditional epic and his knowledge, by now fixed in its major outlines, that the modern world had rendered epic obsolete, he noted on March 27, 1881, the possibility of "a Homeric Ballad, in which Napoleon is a sort of Achilles," only to reject it as glorifying the individual self. Within a few days he added another note in quite a different tenor: "Mode for a historical Drama. Action mostly automatic; reflex movement, etc. Not the result of what is called *motive*, though always ostensibly so, even to the actors' own consciousness. Apply an enlargement of these theories to, say, 'The Hundred Days'!" An Achilles could not move automatically, by reflex; and Hardy's adoption of "human automatism, or impulsion" as a philosophical scheme for *The Dynasts* is traceable as far back as February 16, 1882. For Hardy, historians who emphasized "events and tendencies" as "rivers of voluntary activity" were deceiving themselves, and were even practising charlatanry; "unconscious propensity" counted for far more than "motive."[14]

Yet, if Napoleon were to be denied free will in any significant sense, Hardy would have to provide a credible alternative, a reason for acting that would hold a reader's interest more than a drugged compulsion. This problem, which Hardy perhaps never satisfactorily solved, involved the relationship between an individual's belief that he controlled his destiny and the deterministic conviction of the late Victorian era that effects moved sluggishly but determinedly from specific, if badly understood, causes. He toyed with two schemes: one, an outline of *The Dynasts* in which Napoleon might be represented as haunted "by an Evil Genius or Familiar, whose existence he has to confess to his wives"; the other, in which Napoleon, possessing an insight "by means of necromancy," might see the thoughts of opposing generals.[15] These were inventions, unrelated to any actual Napoleonic folklore (of which, indeed, there is remarkably little in the poem, as Ruth A. Firor points out[16]); and Hardy, in a letter to Mr. Justice J. S. Udal dated December 5, 1915, admitted that he had never systematically studied "Folk Lore."[17] They were quickly rejected as crude oversimplifications.

About this time, too, Hardy, aware that the poem he contemplated would be a long one (as indeed it was: *The Dynasts* is almost as long as the *Iliad*), noted Addison's analysis of Milton's description of Paradise. Following Aristotle, Milton had lavished "all the ornaments of diction on the weak, inactive parts of the fable." The variety of metres that Hardy employed in *The Dynasts* suggests that he kept Addison's note in mind. Hardy agreed with Coleridge that a long poem should not attempt to be poetical "all through." Or, as a modern scholar has rephrased the requirement, the verse of a long poem must not "be so interesting in itself as to be peculiar, and to fatigue the reader by its peculiarities. It must be forgettable as well as memorable. Blank verse has proved very successful in this respect. The line is long enough not to be restless, in the first place. It is long enough and may be simple enough to fade out of the consciousness as verse, and makes its impression as speech."[18]

For a long poem that would employ the human race as a cast of characters; that he planned to treat in a detachedly mocking manner; and that would illustrate the superiority of Will to individual aspirations, Hardy required the largest of canvases. On September 21, 1889, he wrote, "A spectral tone must be adopted. . . . Royal ghosts."[19] And he added the note—"Title: 'A Drama of Kings' "—which, many years later, convinced Hoxie N. Fairchild[20] that he had been reading Robert Buchanan.

Hardy could not have been unaware of Robert Buchanan's *The Drama of Kings*, published in 1871; but that work was a literary performance vastly inferior in imaginative scope to the epic-drama that Hardy contemplated, and Buchanan had little to say about the English contribution to the overthrow of Napoleon. By the early 1890's, Hardy, who had successively selected the historical decade he wanted to treat, his *dramatis personae*, his tone of voice, the scale of the poem, and his philosophic doctrine, knew that he wanted to reassess in a full-length, serious study the influence and action that the English people had exerted on this crucial decade. He planned to render full justice to "the Great Historical Calamity, or Clash of Peoples, artificially brought about some hundred years ago," as he would write in the first sentence of his Preface to *The Dynasts*. Hence, he would consider at some length the maneuverings of English statesmen in the Old House of Commons; the probity of Prime Ministers and the weakness of the reigning sovereign; the tactical brilliance of Nelson and Wellington; the deep-rooted, almost instinctive patriotism of the people at home, arming to resist invasion, and always conscious of Boney's threat to their existence as a free nation; the determination of English soldiers and sailors to do their duty. It would offer, in scene after scene, evidence of how Napoleon's schemes for domination of the Continent had been parried, frustrated, and ultimately ruined by the weight of

English gold and the sacrifice of English lives. It would be, in the best sense, a patriotic treatment of a great moment in national history, one which had been taken largely for granted by English poets prior to Hardy's time.[21]

Hardy did not intend to allow national pride to distort the record, and some of his English characters would show up as sorry human beings. He planned to transcribe conversations of historical personages from historical sources, or to make them consonant with the known characters of these personages. He would consult "oral tradition, accessible scenery, and existing relics," the historian, the biographer, and the journalist.

But England, like France, was subject to a higher Necessity. On April 26, 1890, Hardy made up his mind that the Prime Cause or Invariable Antecedent should be identified by a neuter gender ("It"), and Its doings recounted. As he finished *Tess of the d'Urbervilles*, he contemplated the distance from the events of his drama that he wished to take: "A Bird's-Eye View of Europe at the beginning of the Nineteenth Century. . . . A Drama of the Times of the First Napoleon."[22] The final shape was emerging slowly from his broodings: "Forces; emotions, tendencies. The characters do not act under the influence of reason."[23]

The bitter outcry against *Jude the Obscure*, which Hardy found both unfair and tiresome, made possible the writing of *The Dynasts*, a work to which he now turned full attention. His characters were to include "Burke, Pitt, Napoleon, George III., Wellington . . . and many others." In the sixth decade of his life, he found himself ready for a major statement of belief and the creation of a major work of art, one for which his entire career had served as prologue. All things conspired now to make their presence known, and to contribute to the richness of his epic-drama. The form of that work now merits our attention.

CHAPTER FOUR

Some Notes on the Sublime

THE FORE SCENE of *The Dynasts* introduces us to a mode of visualization which Hardy carries through for the remaining 130 scenes. Europe, the scene of Napoleon's posturings, is personified, created whole and sensate:

> The nether sky opens, and Europe is disclosed as a prone and emaciated figure, the Alps shaping like a backbone, and the branching mountain-chains like ribs, the peninsular plateau of Spain forming a head. Broad and lengthy lowlands stretch from the north of France across Russia like a grey-green garment hemmed by the Ural mountains and the glistening Arctic Ocean.
>
> The point of view then sinks downwards through space, and draws near to the surface of the perturbed countries, where the peoples, distressed by events which they did not cause, are seen writhing, crawling, heaving, and vibrating in their various cities and nationalities.

This passage, as well as dozens like it, is evidence of Hardy's understanding of the contribution that space—a greatness of dimension—makes to the sublime.

Hardy, intimately familiar with Burke's aesthetics, was a personal friend of John Morley, who had written a book about Burke in 1867, and of Leslie Stephen, who had included a perceptive study of Burke in his *History of English Thought in the Eighteenth Century*, which appeared in 1876. Hardy paraphrased Burke in *Far from the Madding Crowd*, and identified for Rebekah Owen[1] the passage in which he defined delight as "mere ease after torment," an echo of Part I, ii-iv, of Burke's *A Philosophical Enquiry into the Origin of our Ideas of the Sublime and Beautiful*. The novelist's concept of style as something that achieves its sublimity in large measure through ruggedness, negligence, darkness, and gloom is traceable to Part III, xxvii.[2] And the vast wastes of Egdon Heath, particularly as described in the opening chapter of *The Return of the Native*, fulfill the definitions of Infinity and Difficulty that Burke had recorded in his celebrated treatise:

... The face of the heath by its mere complexion added half an hour to evening; it could in like manner retard the dawn, sadden noon, anticipate the frowning of storms scarcely generated, and intensify the opacity of a moonless midnight to a cause of shaking and dread. ...

The place became full of a watchful intentness now; for when other things sank brooding to sleep the heath appeared slowly to awake and listen. Every night its Titanic form seemed to await something; but it had awaited thus, unmoved, during so many centuries, through the crises of so many things, that it could only be imagined to await one last crisis—the final overthrow. ...

Haggard Egdon appealed to a subtler and scarcer instinct, to a more recently learnt emotion, than that which responds to the sort of beauty called charming and fair.

The dichotomy of "sublime" and "beautiful" appealed to Hardy, and his epithets for this "home of strange phantoms," without exception, find their artistic justification in Burke's monograph: "obscurity" in the air and in the land, "the chastened sublimity of a moor," "wild regions," "singularly colossal and mysterious in its swarthy monotony," "a lonely face, suggesting tragical possibilities," and "heathy, furzy, briary wilderness." The terror of the unknown, which strikes us all the more forcefully because we may not measure or domesticate the world of the reddleman and of Eustacia Vye, is one great source of the sublime.[3]

With *The Dynasts*, Hardy has moved beyond a simple concept of terror, which has its limitations and perhaps too strong an affinity for Gothic effects. His concern with power—the power that the Immanent Will possesses and exerts unthinkingly—is matched by an alarm that perhaps only poets can imagine fully. The Power of rapine and destruction, of violence and unmanageable fierceness, of a Will which does not care one way or the other

51

how human destinies resolve themselves: before this power men must draw back with horror. What Burke wrote about the Christian God applies with some modifications, to Hardy's non-Christian Will: "But whilst we contemplate so vast an object, under the arm, as it were, of almighty power, and invested upon every side with omnipresence, we shrink into the minuteness of our own nature, and are, in a manner, annihilated before him. And though a consideration of his other attributes may relieve in some measure our apprehensions; yet no conviction of the justice with which it is exercised, nor the mercy with which it is tempered, can wholly remove the terror that naturally arises from a force which nothing can withstand."[4] Hardy, who, as we have seen, denied attributing malevolence to the Immanent Will, also denied it any sense of justice and mercy. His sense of wonderment, commingled with despair, makes for a peculiarly modern sublimity.

There is no precise term for the "long views," which Hardy introduced to his readers long before cinematic techniques provided their equivalent. At any rate, they are Burkean. The world is seen from such magnificent heights that entire armies become snakelike. For example, when describing the Upper Rhine on New Year's Day, after the retreat from Moscow, the debacle at Leipzig, and an English victory in Spain, Hardy writes of dark and grey columns that "glide on as if by gravitation, in fluid figures, dictated by the conformation of the country, like water from a burst reservoir; mostly snake-shaped, but occasionally with batrachian and saurian outlines. In spite of the immensity of this human mechanism on its surface, the winter landscape wears an impassive look as if nothing were happening" (III, IV, i). Tolstoy, in describing the sweeping vista of a battle, had written of what he imagined from ground-level, even when his perspective as author obviously exceeded that of any of his fictional characters. But Hardy translated into literature what Burke had written as an *aperçu*: that "height is less grand than depth; and that we are more struck at looking down from a precipice, than at looking up at an object of equal height. . . ."[5]

Hardy is creating a poem of magnificent largeness, of a relatedness between nations of a Europe that, in Napoleon's time, took weeks to traverse. Every human being, for all that he is one of "Life's queer mechanics," has taken on a power to affect the happiness of generations yet unborn, in lands nearby or across the sea. "War-geared humanity" has never been so described in English poetry. The vision is spectacularly imaged: Mannheim, near the junction of the Rhine and the Neckar, seen from a great heart as "a human head in a cleft stick" (III, IV, ii); the armies of the Allies advancing "like slowworms through grass" (III, VI, i); and, after the slaughter of Waterloo, Europe's lowlands as "a grey green garment half-thrown off, and the sea around like a disturbed bed" on which the figure of Europe lies (After Scene).

The fact that this work, as a "panoramic" achievement, pleased Meredith, a man whose opinion Hardy respected, did not prevent Hardy from admitting that it was a performance "hugely defective." But Stonehenge, too, had required immense force and labor to construct, and Burke's suggestion that the rudeness of the work increases its grandeur, that dexterity produces a strikingly different sort of effect (Part II, xii), applies with special force to *The Dynasts*. We must reconsider the unusual problems that Hardy faced in mortaring his gigantic, rude masses of material.

Emma Clifford, in a suggestive note about Hardy's technique, says that "there are pages in the work in which the numerous facts and anecdotes suggest a catalogue or list. . . . But the reader must catch any small piece of information at the time at which it is given because, except in rare instances, each factual detail in *The Dynasts* is mentioned on one occasion only and we do not hear of it again."[6] She adds that the succession of historical facts leads to "a certain vagueness," and quotes Hardy's disclaimer in his Preface that one should not make an effort to find in his chronicle-piece a "completely organic structure of action, and closely webbed development of character and motive, which are demanded in a drama strictly self-contained."

Hardy chose the dramatic form, as he explained in the *Times Literary Supplement* in a debate which raged during January and February of 1904, because no other form would readily allow of the necessary compression of time and space.[7] His subject cried for direct treatment. Once, when the *Fortnightly Review* asked for his favorite pieces of poetry, Hardy selected Shelley's "Lament" as the most beautiful English lyric, and *Childe Harold* as the best descriptive poetry: "I know this is an old-fashioned taste," he wrote in reply to the editor, "but it is a well-considered relapse on my part, for though in past years I have been very modern, in this matter I begin to feel that mere intellectual subtlety will not hold its own in time to come against the straightforward expression of good feeling."[8] If we keep in mind Hardy's anxiety to be straightforward, we can minimize much of the concern over genre which has marked past discussions of *The Dynasts*. Hardy, like any artist of integrity, did not consider himself a mere imitator of what had gone before. His personal eye, his peculiar moods, established his "style" and determined the form in which he would work.[9] On another occasion he stressed the need for "original treatment" of high tragedy resulting from the "collision between the individual and the general": "treatment which seeks to show Nature's unconsciousness not of essential laws, but of those laws framed merely as social expedients by humanity, without a basis in the heart of things. . . ."[10]

Hence, he could not agree with Zola that literature is measurable by scientific instruments. Art, as he understood it, is science with an addition, just as the materials of fiction are human nature and circumstances. "The Science of Fiction is contained in that large work, the cyclopaedia of life," he declared. "A sight for the finer qualities of existence, an ear for the 'still sad music of humanity,' are not to be acquired by the outer senses alone, close as their powers in photography may be. . . . To see in half and quarter views the whole picture, to catch from a few bars the whole tune, is the intuitive power that supplies the would-be story-writer with the scientific bases for his pursuit."[11]

The Dynasts derives much of its power from the way in which Hardy solved the difficulties confronting him when, with all his memories, his literary sources, his notes, and his grand intentions, he began to write. He had, after all, to superimpose his own ideas of thematic order upon a decade that witnessed important events in cities as far apart as London and Moscow; military and naval triumphs that were partial for both Napoleon and his enemies (battles won or lost at great expense of life failed to settle decisively the events of the following year); the shifting of alliances, the defection of friendly nations, the diplomatic shuffling that confused even those who were in the best position to judge true intentions; an enormous cast (eighty speaking characters in Part First; approximately 125 in each of the next two parts), essential if the full scope of Napoleon's projects was to be made manifest; a variety of moods for which an astonishing variety of meters (thirty, not to mention the blank verse and the deeply rhythmical prose[12]) would be used; and the fact that for one extremely important war of this period, the Peninsular Campaign, Napoleon's failure to be physically present diminished Hardy's chances for unifying his narrative.

The disorder of these diverse materials is, and was to Hardy, *magnificent* in Burke's sense. Confusion of splendid or valuable things in itself can become splendid. "The starry heaven, though it occurs so very frequently to our view, never fails to excite an idea of grandeur," wrote Burke (Part II, xiii). "This cannot be owing to any thing in the stars themselves, separately considered. The number is certainly the cause. The apparent disorder augments the grandeur, for the appearance of care is highly contrary to our ideas of magnificence. Besides, the stars lye in such apparent confusion, as makes it impossible on ordinary occasions to reckon them. This gives them the advantage of a sort of infinity." Hardy was more successful in unifying some parts of his epic-drama than others. When he wrote of events that moved toward some great and plausible conclusion, when the shaping pressures of history (or of the Immanent Will) made clear sense to him, *The Dynasts* fairly sings with the pleasure that craftsman and artifact experience when they confront each other.

After a slow start, Part First achieves exactly this sort of pleasure. It describes the events of a ten-month period: March, 1805 (when Napoleon, already proclaimed Emperor at Notre Dame, repeats the ceremony at Milan, where he takes unto himself the crown of Lombardy) to January, 1806 (when Pitt dies). Three major events form the nucleus of this section: the invasion plans against England, which must be abandoned in August when a demoralized Villeneuve sails for the south; the great battle in October, "sou'-west of Cadiz Bay," of "dead Nelson and his half-dead crew" and "his foes from near and far"; and the two pitched battles of Ulm (in October) and Austerlitz (in December) which establish Napoleon's greatness as military tactician even while Trafalgar robs him forever of the chance for naval supremacy. Hardy, as patriot, made sure that Napoleon's first engagement was with the traditional enemy, England, and that it would mount in excitement as Parliamentarians debated and the people mobilized; that both great empires would recognize the dimensions of the crisis; and that the Emperor of France, deeply moved by the challenge to his ambitions, would bring to bear his entire resources.

Nelson, the counterpart of Villeneuve, is depicted as more than the boy-hero of English legend; he is a man of haggard countenance, the only one who has "pierced the real project of Napoleon," and who has "warnings, warnings," that his "effective hours are shortening here." Anticipating the moment when "Gunner Death" will finish him, Nelson moves forward to his final glory. He is a troubled man, aware, within his breast, of dying fires, and (to an extent that may surprise some readers) condemnatory of himself for days of happiness spent at Naples and Palermo.

> He who is with himself dissatisfied,
> Though all the world find satisfaction in him,
> Is like a rainbow-coloured bird gone blind,
> That gives delight it shares not. (I, II, i)

So much is at stake in this projected invasion, so close the issue, so possible Napoleon's success, that the first large movement of *The Dynasts* is traced for three full acts. In each one Hardy shows how Englishmen, despite political differences, meet Pitt's somber challenge:

> The strange fatality that haunts the times
> Wherein our lot is cast, has no example.
> Times are they fraught with peril, trouble, gloom;
> We have to mark their lourings, and to face them. (I, I, iii)

The stirring scenes of Trafalgar follow. England, more than any other nation of "that so famed year Five," emerges with honor from its struggles against the tyrant. It does not falter or compromise. Perhaps within the poem Napoleon's tirades against England[13] are more insistent on the importance of that nation to French ambitions than they actually were at that particular period of history; but Hardy's emphasis of England as the Emperor's obsession, and of Napoleon's fulminations against the "slim selfish mollusk in its shell" that prevents him from achieving complete triumph, is meant to unify the "splendid confusion" of historical events. Pitt's final illness appropriately rounds off the crowded period Hardy has been considering, and leads inevitably to Part Second. To Pitt, as to England, the location of Austerlitz is as fruitlessly curious a question as the longitude and situation of a cemetery might be to a corpse; but the significance of a "vast adventuring army" "set free" to turn "unhindered strength" against the English cannot be mistaken.

The failure of the King to allow Pitt his Coalition Cabinet was to prove costly in the years ahead; but Hardy does not blame an individual action, or even a fault of character, for the madness which ensued. Much of Part Second remained intractable to the needs of artistic unity. It covers a seven-year period, between 1806 and the invasion of Russia in 1812, during which time Napoleon's enemies were unable to unite, or even to inflict one serious blow against a man who had so obviously overextended his lines of supply. The grandeur inherent in multitude seldom transcends the disorder in this central section of Hardy's epic-drama. Napoleon, as a problem to European statesmen, was momentarily insoluble; he defeated the Prussians at Jena, and negotiated with the Tsar in a way that might put Machiavel to school; he was clearly aware of the host of details he had to master if his imperial schemes were to succeed; and though he trusted his intuition with insufficient skepticism, each passing hour, with its infinitude of chesslike problems, made him more mature, better able to face the morrow. Impressive even at his most petulant, he had become a power to be reckoned with. Yet for purposes of art he is involved in too many schemes: the directing of the Austrian campaign and the battle of Walcheren, the triflings of Spanish government, the attempt to secure dynastic continuity by fathering a male heir. As a result, Hardy's subject-matter never focuses for more than a few pages at a time. Acts II, III, and VI of Part Second, as well as two brief scenes in Act IV, show—fitfully—the campaign that rages, or attenuates, from the Pyrenees to western Spain. But that campaign seems a distraction from weightier matters, and diffuseness is the result. Napoleon's successes (his seven fat years, if we wish to call them so) make Hardy's use of various kinds of irony less effective than they are elsewhere in the poem. Tragic irony, after all, compensates for the transient pleasures of surprise, and thus far Napoleon is not a tragic figure. The Spirits may look ahead to Napoleon's undoing, and foresee at the Emperor's moment of greatest triumph that his reckoning will be bitter; but their predictions of Napoleon's *peripeteia* wear thin while the Emperor persists in astonishing his friends and defeating his enemies. If nothing succeeds like success, and if the protracted time-span prevents the concentration of impact that a single great event can provide, there is little in Napoleon's situation to encourage the ironic superiority of spectators: either of the gods, who alone can be spectators in the world, or of the readers who, knowing all or almost all, think of themselves as gods.[14]

In Part Third Hardy makes clear that Napoleon is no longer able to join judgment with luck. From the crossing of the banks of the Nieman, near Kowno, which launches the invasion of Russia (June, 1812), to the disaster of Waterloo (June, 1815), the number of events treated is severely limited, the development almost linear. Hardy does not need to follow Napoleon's career after the humiliating scene at Bossu: to record Napoleon's return to Paris, his second abdication, his appeal to the Prince Regent ("I came, like Themistocles, to appeal to the hospitality of the British people"), and the final voyage to Saint Helena, the island on which he was to die six years later (May 5, 1821) at the age of fifty-two. The triad of years dramatized in Part Third is in some ways as unified as a morality play.

Hardy's impatience with the extraordinary run of luck that Napoleon has had shows clearly from the beginning, when the Emperor's horse stumbles and throws him. "The portent is an ill one, Emperor," the Spirit of the Years whispers in his ear; and Napoleon acknowledges that he has but "scant years for war." The notes are somber, whenever struck. Time seems curiously compressed as the poem hurtles ahead to Napoleon's damnation; as the *Grande Armée*, a lost tribe of the nineteenth century, returns across the pitiless Russian land it has ravaged. Unimaginable horrors grow out of encounters between determined patriots protecting their homeland and dispirited soldiers who must cross Beresina after Beresina.

59

Part Third is, above all, Napoleon's story. The effrontery of the man who invaded Muscovy with 600,000 men because "circumstance" compelled him; who gilded the dome of the Invalides "in best gold leaf, and on a novel pattern" to distract the Parisians from the massacre of the troops he left behind in eastern Europe; and who succumbs to "life's curse" at Waterloo, holds our shocked attention for scene after scene. He is never out of mind: not during the scenes on the plain of Vitoria or in the Pyrenees which wind up the Peninsular campaign, or at the fête given at Vauxhall Gardens to celebrate Wellington's victory, or in the apartments of the Empress in Paris, or in the bedchamber of the dying Josephine. This section of *The Dynasts* grows grimmer as the list of defeats, slaughters, and defections lengthens. Napoleon's downfall, indeed, is a complicated matter, not easily ascribed to any one cause; but all events during this three-year period conspire against him, and his collapse will occupy the full attentions of the poet in Acts VI and VII. The Waterloo of these Acts serves to counterpoint the Trafalgar of Act V in Part First, and to conclude the record of a man's discovery that the self-made apotheosis of Milan Cathedral (I, VI) cannot endure; similarly, Wellington becomes Napoleon's human counterpart, just as the weaving web of the Immanent Will, the "long while aforetime-figured mesh" of something that Napoleon can only identify as "History," finally destroys him as Nemesis.

While Hardy moves toward the moment when the Emperor can brood that he has become a "miss-mark," he records the talk of men and women in widely separated nations and ties together the inexorable pressures that, with time, will serve more efficiently than Grouchy's bad timing on the Belgian fields to tear the Emperor from his throne. Even if Napoleon's return momentarily elates those who have never lost faith, the Hundred Days are foredoomed. A return to the old, simple belief in the Napoleonic icon has become impossible for a nation still suffering from the mortal blow of the Russian campaign. For the conclusion lay in the beginning, and Napoleon, in his quarters at Charleroi, must live through a midnight of dark omen and wild surmise. In a heavy, tormented sleep he sees a vision of "hundreds of thousands of skeletons and corpses in various stages of decay," "the flesh dropping from them" (III, VI, iii). And, after Ney's thrice unsuccessful charge against the British center, the rest is massacre, and he must meet his "hideous hour" alone in the wood at Bossu.

The tone of this last section does much to unify the disparate scenes, the shifting locales, the varied characters: a tone of increasing gloom as the inevitable comes to be exactly as prefigured in Part First; of an accumulating certainty that Spain, Russia, and Leipzig must lead to the Waterloo of even a greater military leader than Napoleon; of a hardening awareness that man's life is all of a piece, and that here we have a fine example of how public disaster can parallel personal failure (the betrayal of Marie Louise, the death of Josephine, the inner doubts that the future can be hammered into submission by private will).

Yet it would be a serious error to conclude that Hardy's architecture has brought more than a tentative order to this rubble of historical materials, which one Hardy scholar has called "a chaotic mountain waste, hardly yet quarried."[15] The miracle of *The Dynasts* is its infinite variety, not its singleness of theme or tone. Because the subject, in a general sense, was familiar to everyone, Hardy wrote in his Preface that some foreknowledge was assumed necessary "to fill in the junctions required to combine the scenes into an artistic unity." He did what he could to insure that each scene would have a beginning, a middle, and an end. He exhibited characters in pairs and as contrasts, demonstrating his familiarity with the Shakespearean principle of "mirror scenes," the small scenes that use minor characters to show how the actions of princes affect the state. But he could not make —he did not want to make—everything in his epic-drama crystal-clear and simple. The God's plenty of this poem reminds us of what one spectator says during the review of the English and

Hanoverian artillery, cavalry, and infantry at Weymouth: "What a mampus o' folk it is here to-day! And what a time we do live in, between wars and wassailings, the goblin o' Boney, and King George in flesh and blood!" (I, II, iv) It is a world of kings and rustics, of loyal soldiers and cowardly deserters, of disinterested statesmen and ambitious politicians, of high tragedy and opera bouffe. It is, in several important respects, as complex, as darkly rendered, as impossible to understand, as life itself.

Burke believed, and Hardy in his practice demonstrated, that poetry often derives its power from an obscurity "properly conveyed." "It is our ignorance of things that causes all our admiration," wrote Burke (Part II, iv), "and chiefly excites our passions. Knowledge and acquaintance make the most striking causes affect but little. It is thus with the vulgar, and all men are as the vulgar in what they do not understand. The ideas of eternity, and infinity, are among the most affecting we have, and yet perhaps there is nothing of which we really understand so little, as of infinity and eternity." For, of all the elements in *The Dynasts* which bespeak Hardy's effort to achieve poetical sublimity, the Immanent Will is undoubtedly the most important. Behind historical events this superior, non-human, grimly real force personifies what we can never wholly know; our intimations of Its nature are that, no more, *intimations*; and the Will in action is a fearsome thing because It represents the sum of all wills. Human beings assume themselves free in their individual actions; but they are not free; they are compelled to perform in a certain manner; they must play to the end the part they have assumed for themselves. How are we to interpret this? As dark, confused truth. In Burke's epigram, a clear idea is another name for a little idea. The Immanent Will, in essence, is incomprehensible, and an epic-drama which depends on such a "terrible uncertainty" for its central metaphor must be read and evaluated as poetry.

The Will weaves Its "eternal artistries in Circumstance," and, according to the Spirit of the Years, is more concerned with patterns than with their consequence (Fore Scene). Human beings may be tiresome, and may commit "bad mad acts of severance," but the Will, which Hardy did not intend to resemble any anthropomorphic creation of the human race, is not, as a consequence, disenchanted. When a "new and penetrating light" descends upon a given spectacle, "a seeming transparency" results; all men and things exhibit "as one organism the anatomy of life and movement in all humanity and vitalized matter included in the display." The "anatomy" shows waves that bear men's forms along, interrelating threads "which complicate with some, and balance all."

This exhibition of what the Will looks like is always a special effect, awe-inspiring in its very indeterminacy, its fancifulness as vision. Once, after Napoleon has reconfirmed his Emperorship in what the Spirit of the Pities calls a "vulgar stroke of vauntery," the Spirit of the Years shows once more to his "sceptic" colleagues "the preternatural transparency," "as it were the interior of a brain which seems to manifest the volitions of a Universal Will, of whose tissues the personages of the action form portion" (I, I, vi). Again, above the field of Austerlitz, the Semichoruses of the Pities call upon the "Great Necessitator" to "quicken the issue" and "dull to suffering" those who must die; but this cry angers the Spirit of the Years because the Semichoruses misunderstand the "Eternal Urger," and he shows his kindred Spirits once more this singular vision of the "brain-like network of currents and ejections, twitching, interpenetrating, entangling, and thrusting hither and thither the human forms" (I, VI, iii). Napoleon's schemings for a free road to Asia and the end of "English merchant-mastership in Ind" will crumble with the "bleached skeletons" of his army; and, much later in the poem, the Spirit of the Years again acts as conjuror to show, in "the unnatural light" which "usurps that of the sun," "the films of brain-tissues of the Immanent Will, that pervade all things, ramifying through the whole army, *Napoleon* included, and moving them to Its inexplicable artistries" (III, I, i). At the whirlwind of Waterloo, we behold Wellington, like Napoleon in earlier visions of the Will, as part of the interconnecting tissue, "acting while discovering his intention to act." Hardy adds: "By the lurid light the faces of every row, square, group, and column of men, French and English, wear the expression of those of people in a dream." This sight disturbs the Spirit of the Pities, who, in tremulous tones, urges the Spirit of the Years to reveal the transparency "no more" (III, VII, vii).

This apparition, which Hardy describes as a glowing tissue of nerves and fibers in which human beings are inextricably entangled, cannot become more specific or hard in its outline. It is appropriate that the Spirit of the Years shows "the rapt Determinator" to the younger Spirits much in the fashion of a prestidigitator. There is, indeed, something magical about the Immanent Will, something that the human mind can perceive only through the approximations of language. Though the unearthly light may be stressed on one occasion and not another, though we see Wellington more sharply in the final revelation than ever before, the Will itself, "the Great Foresightless," is not to be defined precisely.

The Immanent Will, as a reading of the universe, cannot be distorted into anything sanguine; but more needs to be said about the degree of Its cheerlessness, if only because such assessment indicates how far we have come from Milton's concept of epic. For the moment, however, let me repeat that the chief value of *The Dynasts* does not rest with the observations made by the Spirits, or with the deterministic philosophy that they expound, but with the epic-drama's scope; its sublimity arising from several of the sources that Burke so ably defined in 1757, and enlarged upon in his second edition of the *Enquiry* in 1759; and with Hardy's greatness of intention. The poet here was attempting to define the nature of man's relation to unknown and unknowable forces, and doing so confident in the belief that each poet must write his own definition and abide by it. These Spirits serve the Immanent Will despite their questions and doubts because it is inconceivable that they should not. We as readers can believe in their obedience not only because the Immanent Will is a concept of some importance among Hardy's contemporaries and whatever the Spirits do is consistent with that concept, but because such obedience is essential to both the meaning and the magnitude of *The Dynasts*.

CHAPTER FIVE

The Dynasts and Paradise Lost

THE STORY of the war with Napoleon, which takes three parts and nineteen acts to unfold, may seem to be the story of a small war, at least so far as many readers inured to the horrors of our century are concerned. Monism has become old-fashioned in a cosmos dominated by Einstein's dogma. Nevertheless, my faith that *The Dynasts* is an unread great poem of our age, perhaps the greatest poem, is related to my strong feeling that it affords us the only possible modern version of what for several hundred years was regarded as the best of all literary genres: the epic.

Not all readers of this poem are in agreement, however, and some have used elaborate machinery to reach what seems to me the wrong conclusion. Whether *The Dynasts* can be acted on a literal stage—or cannot be acted (the latter view is usually preferred)—is a question that excites considerations of form; but Hardy explicitly said that his work was a frank divergence from classical and other dramatic precedent. Another frequently made comparison, with Goethe's *Faust*, based on the fact that certain scenes in both poems take place in regions beyond mortal ken, is temporarily arresting, but ultimately fortuitous: *The Dynasts* lacks both a Margaret and Mephistopheles. Another critic has compared the poem to an oratorio, and we can well agree that it is petty to demand information on where Hardy's Spirits enter from, that it is far simpler to assume they are always present on-stage, much as singers at an oratorio—but this observation turns out to be still another attempt to define the form of *The Dynasts*; moreover, the same critic's attempt to see a parallel in *Passion*, a medieval French play by Arnoul Greban which Hardy never read (by the critic's own admission), is, for obvious reasons, unpromising.[1]

Hardy gave a clue to his poem's most important aspect when

he labeled it "an epic-drama." There are Miltonic overtones to his ubiquitous irony. Much had happened to the epic tradition since 1667, and the question of form inevitably led him to the consideration of meaning. Hardy's recognition of the change manifests itself in a work which radically modifies the Miltonic relationship between man and God in at least three ways: the celestial machinery, which Hardy chose to invent rather than borrow; the pitiful stature of Napoleon as opposed to the genuine majesty of Adam; and the inability of *The Dynasts* to promise a happy ending.

Before we consider these in detail, however, we may note that "epic-drama" does have historical antecedents in English literature, and that Milton himself was familiar with the concept. In the celebrated digression that opens the Second Book of *The Reason of Church Government Urged against Prelaty* (1641-42), Milton has recorded his indecision about the kind of great poem he intended to write: "whether that epic form whereof the two poems of Homer, and those other two of Virgil and Tasso, are a diffuse, and the book of Job a brief model: or whether the rules of Aristotle herein are strictly to be kept, or nature to be followed, which in them that know art, and use judgment, is no transgression, but an enriching of art. . . ." Milton wanted to keep the best features of both traditions, if possible. *Paradise Lost* would have been a drama if the Renaissance had not held in higher esteem the epic form, and if Milton had not outgrown his original outline of the biblical story in *Adam Unparadised*, recorded in some detail by 1642 as a "tragedy." But Milton thought in dramatic terms even after he chose the epic as his medium. His absorption with the dramatic principle of conflict animates the great two books which open his "poem in twelve books," and drama is the essence of the double theme of war against God in Heaven and war against God on earth. *Paradise Lost* itself is an example of epic-drama.

Milton's preference for blank verse over the heroic couplet may have been unusual in his time, and his defense does have a belligerent tone: "The Measure is English Heroic Verse without Rime, as that of Homer in Greek, and of Virgil in Latin; Rime being no necessary Adjunct or true Ornament of Poem or good Verse, in longer Works especially, but the Invention of a barbarous Age, to set off wretched matter and lame Meeter. . . . This neglect then of Rime so little is to be taken for a defect, though it may seem so perhaps to vulgar Readers, that it rather is to be esteem'd an example set, the first in English, of ancient liberty recover'd to Heroic Poem from the troublesom and modern bondage of Rimeing." But his subject matter did not surprise his contemporaries. The orthodox Protestant optimism of the age nowhere found a stronger champion. According to this optimism, Man exercised his freedom of choice, which had been given him by a God unwilling to accept mechanical obedience. Man might fall from divine grace (the choice between good and evil presupposed that he knew in advance what evil was and that evil did exist distinct from and in opposition to good) but his fall need not be permanent. Indeed, the human Christ, "one greater Man," would restore him to "the blissful Seat." If anything, his restoration to grace would be to an eminence even higher than the one he had previously enjoyed. In the meantime, he would be watched over by God and all the good angels. His destiny would concern the Heavenly Host. His thoughts would implicate Eve and, more importantly, Eve's creator; his sin would be God's betrayal, but his bliss would be God's bliss.

Such are the commonplaces of Milton criticism, which have rescued us from the heresy of Blake and Shelley and which correctly place emphasis on Adam as hero, Satan as villain, and Christ as Savior. They render explicit what Milton deeply believed: the ending would be happy. In no real sense can it be maintained that Milton wrote tragedy.

> . . . so [Christ] dies,
> But soon revives, Death over him no power
> Shall long usurp; ere the third dawning light
> Returne, the Starres of Morn shall see him rise
> Out of his grave, fresh as the dawning light,
> Thy ransom paid, which Man from death redeems,
> His death for Man, as many as offer'd Life
> Neglect not, and the benefit imbrace
> By Faith not void of workes: this God-like act
> Annuls thy doom, the death thou shouldst have dy'd,
> In sin for ever lost from life. . . . (XII, 419-429)

The spirit of life is upon Man, "immortal Life"; the head of Satan will be bruised, and his "two maine armes," Sin and Death, will meet defeat.

We wrong Milton if in disclaiming the tragic intention we see nothing but sweetness and light. Milton fully recognized the bitterness of the struggle between the Heavenly Host and the powers ranged behind "th' Apostate Angel"; but, more important, Milton foresaw a blinding triumph, a final victory which would Christianize his epic. (The emphasis on cosmic elements increased as Milton developed his outline for *Adam Unparadised* into an epic.) Moreover, everything we know of Milton's personal life confirms the impression that he thought man himself to be worthy. The dignity of man is the basic postulate of his philosophy, its bone and pith. Adam and Eve, despite their fault, are heroic, figures worthy of an epic.

The Dynasts, however, does not envision the stable universe that Milton knew. Neither Ptolemy nor Copernicus had much to do with the making of Hardy's cosmology: the earth is not significant in terms of relationship to other planets, even the sun, and the Protestant God with his hosanna-singing choir has vanished from the heavens. Instead, species painfully evolve toward an unseeable goal set at a tremendous distance. The Immanent Will, Hardy's substitute for God, is a "viewless, voiceless Turner of the Wheel." "He" has become "It." No longer the "King of Glorie," but the "First or Fundamental Energy," dominates the cosmos. Hardy proudly proclaims that the monistic theory of the universe excludes "the importation of Divine personages from any Mythology as ready-made sources or channels of Causation, even in verse, and excluded the celestial machinery of, say, *Paradise Lost*, as peremptorily as that of the *Iliad* or the *Eddas*" (Preface). His implication is clear. We cannot return to the Bible for our divinities. All anthropomorphism disintegrates, Lucifer equally with Christ, Beelzebub with Michael, Moloch with Raphael; Hardy invents "phantom intelligences," a new celestial machinery. The figures through which Hardy endows his scene with more than ordinary coloration bear names like The Years, The Pities, The Spirits Sinister and Ironic, The Spirit of Rumour, The Shade of the Earth, The Spirit Messengers, and The Recording Angels.

As imaginative creations they contribute to the sublime effect that Hardy wanted to create; these inhabitants of the Otherworld are more carefully characterized than a hasty first reading might indicate. The Spirit of the Years acts as senior citizen, and, as Bailey shows,[2] can look unmoved on Death because so much of his doctrine is Stoic; determinist though he may be, he opposes war; the range of his prophecies is limited, and he is far from omniscient. He depends on the facts of experience, and neglects the instincts of feeling.

More likely Hardy's deeper commitment was to the Spirit of the Pities, the only one of the Spirits he individualized in his Preface ("impressionable and inconsistent in its views, which sway hither and thither as wrought on by events"). This Spirit is more sensitive to the needs of ailing men than to the demands of Immanent Will, and his resistance, however ineffectual, must be explained by his relative youthfulness: he came into being "in what the earthlings call their Tertiary Age!" (I, I, vi) He commemorates the defeated, the fallen, the unhappy everywhere. He is less concerned with heroism than with men's reactions to the numbing pressure of everyday circumstance, and we will learn little from him about the movements of troops or the strategy which dynasts employ. Many of the things he says are appealingly innocent; he possesses a modest gift of prophecy, a capacity to learn from experience, and even a faith in the future that the other Spirits do not share. For him there exists a possibility that a growing consciousness of man's anguish may lead the Immanent Will some day to enlarge the possibilities of human conduct.

The most complex of the Spirits, however, is the Spirit Ironic. He blames by praising; he emphasizes by saying the opposite of what he means; he understates; he comments by indirection; and sometimes he derisively attacks.[3] Time after time he shows us the absurdity of men behaving as if they controlled destiny. The Spirits themselves cannot prevent from happening what must happen, what they often know in advance will happen. In this sense they resemble Homer's gods who occasionally must yield to a sterner necessity (even Zeus cannot prevent his son from being slain on the field of battle). For this Spirit, irony becomes more than a trick of speech; it is a perspective, a way of beholding life. Scientifically well informed, the Spirit Ironic stresses logic or the intellectual basis of judgment. Bailey reminds us, however, that he "comes close to being a champion of the Pities in the clash of opinion among the Spirits,"[4] and certainly Hardy did not make him mean in temper. The role he plays in relation to the other Spirits and to the Will suggests an interest in, a willingness to care about, human destiny.

The other Spirits incarnate "tendencies." The Spirit Sinister is sketchily blocked in, and seems to stand for a kind of malice and love of evil for its own sake. He approves of the most blackguardly of Napoleon's actions, and admires war for its bloody brutality. But the high ratio of prose to verse in his speeches, and the limited number of lines that Hardy gives to him (fewer than 100) suggest that Hardy was not anxious to expand this particular portrait. Perhaps, also, he considered much of his function dramatically fulfilled by the Spirit Ironic.

Even less may be said about the others. The Spirit of Rumour, like Homer's personified Rumour, has a limited gift of prevision, and avoids becoming involved in the quarrels between individual Spirits. The Spirit-Messengers and the Recording Angels pass on and record the news; they are essentially reporters. The Spirit of the Earth, an "ineffectual Shade" (Fore Scene), sighs unhappily at the wars which ruin her beauty and disturb her serenity.

Hardy's Spirits are aware that they form a Chorus. Moreover, they can instantly evaluate the meaning of any human action. In this significant way they differ from the members of the Chorus in a play by Aeschylus or Sophocles. The writers of classical tragedy used the Chorus to lament the pride of men and women who sought to escape from divinely established patterns; sometimes, too, the Chorus would interpret the will of God. But the dark, even gnomic language of the Chorus betrayed the limitations of the understanding that it possessed, and there was little certainty as to the rightness of the guesses that were made. Knowing more, *aware* of more, the Spirits of Hardy's poem become magnificent instruments of an ironist's intention. They perceive the pity, understand the deterministic principle, and philosophize about the relative scale of human beings in an inhuman universe, with lucidity and breath-taking appropriateness; they are never bewildered by events; they may regret, but they cannot be confused by, the spectacle before their eyes. Their perspective is magnified, cosmic; for many readers in the modern world, true. Some are wiser than others. (The Spirit of the Years establishes as early as the Fore Scene his superiority over his fellow-Spirits.) Their ages are unequal: the Spirit Ironic tells us, in an aside, that the Spirit of the Pities is "a mere juvenile" (I, I, vi). Perhaps they are not immortal. At one point, the Spirit of the Years chides the Chorus of the Pities for criticizing the Immanent Will, which has prolonged the death of Nelson by two hours and fifty minutes:

> Young Spirits, be not critical of That
> Which was before, and shall be after you! (I, V, iv)

Their hierarchy is not an important matter to Hardy, and should not be to his reader. But how different, in all ways, from the celestial machinery of Milton's *Paradise Lost*!

In the transformation of God to Fate, the closeness of Man to God necessarily must suffer. The extent of that severance seems to be the degree to which the epic tradition has undergone significant alteration at Hardy's hands. Adam was "First Man, of Men innumerable ordain'd / First Father" (VIII, 297-298), fit for converse with ambassadors of God, able to rule nobly over the Garden of bliss, and sufficiently knowledgeable to name "Beast, Fish, and Fowle." He is unlike the brutes of the field; he stands erect, and is endowed "with Sanctities of Reason." Grateful for the good which has descended unto him, he willingly worships "God Supream, who made him chief / Of all his works" (VII, 515-516), and who, moreover, has made him in God's similitude.

> Thrice happie men,
> And sons of men, whom God hath thus advanc't,
> Created in his Image, there to dwell
> And worship him, and in reward to rule
> Over his Works, on Earth, in Sea, or Air,
> And multiply a Race of Worshippers
> Holy and just: thrice happie if they know
> Their happiness, and persevere upright. (VII, 625-632)

It is for the wonder of Man—a wonder which manifests the glory of God—that the Empyrean rings with *Halleluiahs* on the Sabbath. And we remember that the "angelic harmonies" that cheered God on His return from the six days of Creation sang clearly of God's intention "to visit oft the dwellings of just Men," and to send "his winged Messengers" frequently to Earth "on errands of supernal Grace."

But Napoleon, the most important single figure in the enormous cast of characters which Hardy assembles, curses his "jail of flesh" and nowhere discovers that peace of mind which Adam before the Fall knew and enjoyed. He can never have spiritual ease. When he crowns himself Emperor, he has little respect for the Pope even as temporal ruler. He honors force, but does not comprehend the moral integrity which makes force meaningful. The higher power that he recognizes through the isinglass of his insatiable ambition is either hostile, in terms of his inability to befriend it, or indifferent. He is, in other words, isolated both from his fellow human beings because of inner greatness and from God because of external insignificance in time. Hardy's undercutting destroys Napoleon's heroism, his heroic aspect, and that of all the people involved in his poem. They are all caught in the midst of forces they do not understand or, at best, sense dimly. Napoleon's knowledge that he has nothing more to lose but life is characteristic of an attitude shared by many of Hardy's figures. The knowledge comes after Waterloo, matches his bitter understanding that he came too late in time "to assume the prophet or the demi-god," and finds brilliant articulation in the Marlovian lines,

> Great men are meteors that consume themselves
> To light the earth. This is my burnt-out hour. (III, VII, ix)

Let us look for a moment more closely at Napoleon, a hero of an epic-drama who is continually belittled by the Spirits, who in large measure lacks freedom of choice, and who acts time and again as a sullen, restless mortal. *The Trumpet-Major*, published in 1880, had explicitly characterized Napoleon as "the mighty little man who was less than human in feeling, and more than human in will"; but that novel, a charming study of country life in southern England rather than a serious exploration of the Napoleonic Wars, did not bring Napoleon on-stage for any scene. The Spirits in *The Dynasts* make explicit the insignificance of Napoleon "in the elementary ages' chart." The reader, who

74

judges god-like on the basis of more information than is available to any single human actor, is encouraged to sneer at Napoleon's pretensions. Dynastic, imperial splendor disintegrates into sordid, mean failure. The Spirit of the Years can say of him, even before the action begins, that his twitchings will "twitch him into his lonely grave" (Fore Scene); and will add, after Waterloo, *"Sic diis immortalibus placet."*

It is a sorry comedown for a man tormented by the knowledge that "Europe's wormy dynasties" will not rerobe themselves in their old gilt, "to dazzle anew the globe." His final words are a half-choked, splenetic outburst against England, whose "tough, enisled, self-centred, kindless craft" was enough, finally, to ruin his "high-doctrined dreams." Nor does he fully understand the nature of the greater forces which have overcome him. He never repudiates his ambitions; instead, he believes that in the world he inhabited they had no chance. He lays great stress upon the faulty timing of his entrance upon the world-stage. The calendar betrayed him before he could establish his successors. At the end of his career, he still has the passion to argue that he found "the crown of France in the mire," and picked it up with the point of his prevailing sword. His life came to nothing, but he *tried*. Nothing in his final soliloquy suggests that he repents; much is there to suggest the magnificence of his misdirected energy.

No human character in the epic-drama knows more about Napoleon than he would have known at the time and in the land in which he judges. If Hardy is consistent about anything, it is this very sense of immediacy. The dominant Present raises genuine problems of interpretation if only because Napoleon, during his lifetime, was not well understood. The reader is being asked to disregard his knowledge of Napoleon's fate, to relive the hopes and anxieties that swayed millions of people who did not have certain knowledge of how the drama would play itself out. As a consequence, Napoleon is talked about as a series of different Napoleons, not all of whom can possibly coexist within the same human frame. Dramatically, then, Hardy's fragmented view of Napoleon carries with it a certain measure of risk: the desire to achieve immediacy, to recreate the historical past as the ever-living Present, means that we are not always sure what Hardy believed about his supreme personage.

It is worth remembering that Napoleon does not immediately appear in *The Dynasts*, and that Hardy first shows us (according to "a sound dramatic principle") how the common people of England and France, Admiral Decrès, the debaters in the Old House of Commons, and the assembled party-goers of London, regard him. Some love him; others fear him; he cannot be *all* they say. In several early scenes he is depicted as a brilliant, nervous, devious, active, self-assured hero, a man convinced of his right to create history. For many, he is the evangel. Likely enough, as one passenger on a stagecoach says, that "Heaven alone, who reads the secrets of this man's heart, can tell what his meaning and intent may be. . . ." (I, I, i) Perhaps this is Hardy's view as well: Napoleon is a complex, strange human being, with an occasional noble motive, more than the Napoleon of historical records, less than the Napoleon of English popular imagination, and, all in all, a man.

Napoleon's goal changes, of course, as opportunity allows; but in several moments of history, and in the poem too, he speaks of his objective as a smashing of the English coalitions which Pitt has established. He talks of freeing from bondage "to a cold manorial caste" a people who await their "liberation." In part his greatness derives from his vision of a Napoleonic Europe, and he is surely no money-seeking adventurer pure and simple. Hardy never denies his brilliance as a general; his firm grasp of strategic realities; his ability to move armies as if they are chessmen. Mistaken Napoleon may be; but part of his anger against England is founded on a conviction that the English speak in cant to disguise the true nature of their Realpolitik. (He calls them "licentious" in II, III, ii, "as all canting people are.") He laughs to scorn the sight of the Russian clergy at Borodino, who carry an image "said to work strange miracles." To him war is pagan in essence, and one cannot hire "the enginry of Heaven" (III, I, iv). He is quick to praise the clever, astute in perceiving the distrust of his lieutenants, more than "the vulgar foe" which General Mack calls him at Ulm. He is, as much as any man can be, the spirit of his nation. His soldiers express their devotion often. When he deserts his men, who are retreating from Russia, the Mad Soldier's song is filled with a tremendous *personal* shock (III, I, xi). When Napoleon returns from exile, he persuades a battalion of a French royalist regiment of the line to join him with a speech that speaks of his sense of identity with France:

> I have thought it out, my friend,
> And value not my life as in itself,
> But as to France, severed from whose embrace
> I am dead already. (III, V, iv)

His skill as a negotiator, most interesting perhaps in the conversation with the Tsar Alexander (II, I, viii), and as a gallant courtier, is admirably depicted. In his desire to found a dynasty he is most human, and Hardy makes clear, and somehow pathetic, his driving passion. The scenes between Napoleon and Josephine, for example, are rendered with delicate understanding, and II, VI, iii, the scene in which Napoleon urges Dubois, the Accoucheur, to save the Empress Marie Louise rather than the baby that she is laboring with such great difficulty to produce, with unmistakable compassion. He is, as a whole, complicated, vain, and ruthless, often unexpectedly weak, more than once a figure to be sympathized with, one who reminds us what a piece of work is a man.

But there is an old irony inherent in his situation, one that marks him off as the very opposite of Milton's Adam. He began as democrat and leveler, and became the thing he overthrew. He was his own worst antagonist; divided within himself, he never understood himself, much less the Immanent Will; he sowed his own seeds of self-destruction. His vision of a Europe confederated beneath his flag may have been splendid, and it certainly ennobled what was otherwise coarse and unbearable about him. Nor was he canting when he spoke of it. But his intentions were shaped by dynastic vanity, and a man who seeks to sweep the world clean with a stiff broom must think of a better foundation for his new order than intermarriage with the House of Hapsburg. His faithlessness to Josephine is, in small, the greedy opportunism in affairs of state which corrodes the faith of his generals. When France wins on the battlefields, his arrogance seems natural; when France no longer believes in him, it becomes trumpery.

The deterioration of Napoleon is shown in images of seediness that remind us of Satan's physical debilitation: the puffed calf (III, I, i); the "red eyes, raw nose, rheumatic manner" at Borodino (III, I, v); the unshaven face within the Kremlin (III, I, viii); the shabby, muddy attire of a returning loser from the Russian campaign (III, I, xii); the heavy sleep at Leipzig (III, III, iv); the haggard, disordered appearance near the Ranstädt gate (III, III, v); the yellow face and the wild eyes at Avignon, after the unsuccessful attempt to commit suicide at Fontainebleau (III, IV, vi); the quivering flesh that reacts to the Declaration of the Allies placing him outside the pale of civil and social relations (III, VI, i); the sweating nightmare of Charleroi (III, VI, iii). It is piquant that the Duke of Wellington and Napoleon should both be forty-six years of age at the Battle of Waterloo; but only Napoleon is shown as old, tired, and depressed. "His elevated face makes itself distinct in the morning light as a gloomy, resentful countenance, blue-black where shaven, and stained with snuff, with powderings of the same on the breast of his uniform. His stumpy figure, being just now thrown back, accentuates his stoutness" (III, VII, ii). He cannot escape terrifying dreams, one of which presents to him a mutilated and bleeding Lannes, saying,

"What—blood again? Still blood?" (III, VII, vi) And in his final appearance, riding a "jaded horse" through the wood of Bossu, he falls asleep in the saddle; "the moon shines upon his face, which is drawn and waxen."

These descriptions, in conjunction with the increasingly frantic and ill-tempered actions that Hardy has selected as symptomatic of Napoleon's last years of command, illustrate a consistent concept of personality. That, in turn, is defined by three factors: wonder at Napoleon's ability to exploit the emotional forces of nationalism; a feeling that this is a man of shadings rather than of blacks and whites; and a knowledge that Napoleon's success would be calamitous for Europe. The Emperor is a man of virtues and vices hopelessly commingled who became hardened to suffering. Whatever he did, one crime or a thousand, received sanctification in the cry, "For France!" He murdered soldiers in the field, and worse still, helpless families who lived in the lands he coveted. As his powers grew, the wastage became more tremendous, his conscience weaker. The universe had already suffered too much on his account by the time of Waterloo; order would have to be restored in a final Armageddon. At the end, although in some ways he falls to lesser men, he is morally isolated; he has blasted the golden opinions of others; he might have been something better, but he has ended as only a failure, one who can say, with justification, that he has nothing more to lose but life.

But Hardy's indictment of Adam's descendants is broader than simply the denunciation of Napoleon as the ruthless manipulator of men. He has little time to spend in praise of Nelson and Pitt, who give to England, through their selflessness, examples of patriotic idealism. A refusal by Fox, the Foreign Secretary, to listen to Guillet de la Gevrillière's offer to assassinate Napoleon, or a moving moment in the field before Coruña, where Sir John Moore dies of his wounds, do not weigh heavily in the balance, which is dragged down by the extraordinary assemblage of kings, queens, and military leaders who believe, like Napoleon, that what they do is politically realistic. The selfish game they play is Napoleon's game. Their desires to aggrandize, to expand national boundaries, to join an alliance with Napoleon when he is up and to rend him when he is down, are desires that Napoleon can fully understand. It is an age of dynasts. Every dynast, while publicly denouncing Napoleon's avarice, secretly envies his success. Hardy demonstrates that Europe for the most part is a jungle of wild animals, and how, if England did not exist, there would be no significant difference between the rumpled flags that Napoleon tears down and the brightly colored ensign that he runs up in their place. The Emperor came to power because the unlamented Bourbons, in their going, created a vacuum. Nobody remembers Marie Antoinette, decaying in a back-garden.

It is impossible for the dynasts to speak truthfully to one another. The Austrian Emperor, Francis, denies having any interest in going to war, and speaks of the "friendship and esteem" that he feels for Napoleon (I, IV, v). Napoleon tells Alexander at the River Nieman that he fought Russia only because it was England's ally (II, I, vii). Alexander, flushed by the prospect of dividing the world with Napoleon, swears eternal friendship (II, I, viii). No dynast can admit frankly his responsibility for the international holocaust. The King of Prussia denies that he provoked a war, and Napoleon blandly blames his ally, the Tsar, only moments after having said to Alexander that in him alone "nobility has shone."

More than any single event, the courtship of Maria Louisa (who, after her marriage, becomes Marie Louise) shows that sentiment cannot interfere with the supposedly "practical." When Napoleon negotiated a series of alliances against England, the Archduchess prophesied that he would die within a year. She hated the French, and sneered at the "bourgeois Corsican," while her Viennese subjects called her a girl of patriotic build. But the French Emperor's determination to send down his "shoots to future time" leads to a coarse proposal at the Arch-Chancellor Cambacérès' ball, negotiations with Metternich, the hysteria of Josephine (who is now repudiated), and the Emperor Francis's cynicism about Napoleon's need for "the spruce commodity" of children. Metternich forces the "fresh-colored, girlish, and smiling" Archduchess to consider the Empire's happiness, and to forget her hatred of Napoleon. She has neither the intelligence nor the will-power to resist her father.

Napoleon, as we know, had been deeply involved in schemes for marrying a member of the Tsar's family, and the alliance with the Austrian dynasty offends the Empress-Mother of Russia, who bitterly tells Alexander that he has been "coolly shelved" (II, V, vii). Even Alexander, who speaks ingenuously about Napoleon as a "friend" who might have loved him better if Anne or Catharine had been plighted successfully to the French Emperor, is embarrassed at the new twist in events. The simultaneous parleying with Russia and Austria, and Napoleon's insulting new alliance with Austria, mean that the marriage will have a short life. As in fact it does. After the battle of Vitoria, which leads to Wellington's field-marshalship, Austria joins an alliance against France, and an attaché can remark, "So much for Napoleon's marriage! I wonder what he thinks of his respected father-in-law now" (III, II, iv).

Why pity Marie Louise? She married not for love, but to provide her father with "a happy doorway" for his "purposings," for "a wide Empire's welfare," for canting reasons that depressed the Spirit of the Years into saying, "The Will must have its way." When the foes of France surrounded Paris, she learned that the French refused to fight to defend her. Why, indeed, should she be surprised?

The character of the dynasts is uniformly depressing in the striking series of speeches of III, IV, viii. At the London Opera House, where the Allied sovereigns celebrate the peace in the Royal Box, the Prince Regent, the Emperor of Russia, and the

King of Prussia discuss the rumors emanating from Elba. The King of Prussia hopes that Napoleon is turning imbecile, but suspects that the gossip is false. "If he is not imbecile," he continues, "he is worse—planning how to involve Europe in another war. It was a short-sighted policy to offer him a home so near as to ensure its becoming a hot-bed of intrigue and conspiracy in no long time!"

The key phrase, an ironic one to Hardy, is "short-sighted policy." All policy pursued by the dynasts is short-sighted, or at best only awkwardly suited to the facts. No emperor, tsar, or king can truly say that his policy succeeds. No people benefit. The European land is overrun by faceless armies who know not why or for whom they fight. The dynasts—the new race of God's children— are limited in their perceptions of why things happen, or how empires grow, or what indeed the phenomenon of Napoleon signifies. This is a sorry, mean family, not evil but graceless; not stupid, but without moral integrity, and unworthy of ruling the world. High ideals should have some importance in the affairs of sovereign nations. The fact that they did not have such importance, except to England and not always there, constituted, for Hardy, the "Great Historical Calamity, or Clash of Peoples, artificially brought about some hundred years ago."

Milton's faith in the Resurrection, in life beyond life, simply does not apply to what the Spirit of the Pities names a "terrestrial tragedy" (Fore Scene). That which Milton held as truth catholic and apostolic becomes truth relative in the speech of the Spirit of the Years:

> A local thing called Christianity,
> Which the wild dramas of the wheeling spheres
> Include, with divers other such, in dim
> Pathetical and brief parentheses,
> Beyond whose span, uninfluenced, unconcerned,
> The systems of the suns go sweeping on
> With all their many-mortaled planet train
> In mathematic roll unceasingly. (I, I, vi)

82

It is true that in Part Third Hardy makes a strong effort to indicate reasonable grounds for hope. The After Scene contains the beautiful prayer of the Semichoruses of the Pities, which looks ahead to the day when "these pale panting multitudes" shall find fulfillment. The Spirit of the Years, in anguish, recalls a time when pity was allowable, before experience convinced him otherwise. There is a hope that "a genial germing purpose" underlies the otherwise meaningless travailings of humanity.

Nevertheless, the epic-drama often seems to confirm the bleak answers of the Spirit of the Years, and to deny support to the naïve, beautiful, and humble questions of the Spirit of the Pities. The Spirits, no less than Napoleon and those whose gyrations are interrelated with his own, are servants of the Immanent Will. The Chorus in I, VI, viii underscores the insignificance of their role. Christianity, which conceives another view of human destiny, is too ceremonial and institutionalized to be recognizable. It has traveled too far from its original "gracious purpose" (I, I, vi). For example, the Spirit of the Pities fails to recognize it at the Cathedral of Milan.

The human race comes out poorly in many of the speeches made by the Spirits. The French crowd which cheers Napoleon's goal of invading England makes "confused and simmering sounds" (I, I, ii). After Nelson's death, the Spirit of the Pities describes human beings as "things mechanized / By coils and pivots" (I, V, iv), and no Spirit more than this one wishes humanity well. The Spirit of the Years, at the *conversazione* of the Marchioness of Salisbury, calls on the Rumours, those "clarionists of human welterings," to describe recent European history. Borodino, a field of "wholesale butchery," provokes the Spirit of the Years to dour reflections on "the mindless minions" of the Will. Is the "unreined" ramping of the "hot-breath'd war-horse" more or less desirable than the "so-called ancient order"? (III, III, vi) The Spirits have no ready answer. Noble blood is hardly sacred. Marie Louise, according to the Spirit Ironic, is the daughter of that "divinely dry and crusted line," the Hapsburgs (II, V, viii); and warfare, "plied by the Managed for the Managers" (III, VII, viii), will ruin her inheritance. The Managed die; but the Managers do not keep their profits either. All matters which have earned the praise of the human race diminish to "incidents and grooves of Earth's unfolding" (III, VII, ix). What Milton once saw as the supreme irony, the death which "slits the thin-spun life" at the moment one thinks to have won "the fair guerdon," is surpassed by Hardy's greater irony: all human fame, all human honors, perish and become a nothingness in the presence of the Will.

The Dynasts does not necessarily present a reader with richer truth or deeper insight than Milton's *Paradise Lost*; but, at the very least, it is closer to contemporary moods. Its recognition that a community of Christian tradition may not be appealed to and that instead a new tradition must find roots abandons (whether rightly or wrongly we still cannot say) the old set of insights. It creates a new cosmology because, unlike *Paradise Lost*, it refuses to depend on biblical revelation. Its gods are as pagan as the war it describes, the war which Hardy himself names pagan. It rejects the philosophy that conflict between good and evil is the fundamental issue of human life. That doctrine cannot be supported by empirical reasoning. *The Dynasts* depicts war as a "mimic fray" (III, I, ii), and its outcome is not important.

The possibility is strong that epic tradition without strongly religious orientation must negate all values. The claim of some critics that Hardy's poem vigorously maintains the dignity of man does not follow logically from the evidence they present, and it is difficult to see how any evidence gathered from the poem would support such a conclusion. The Sardonic rules here. "Power" is a jest mouthed by megalomaniacs. "In the elemental ages' chart," the Spirit of the Years, wisest and oldest of the "phantom intelligences," compares Napoleon to the meanest insect on the obscurest leaf (III, VII, ix). Napoleon controls nothing. Men of cruder intelligence, the obviously inferior successors to Pitt and Fox, chart his defeat. His pretensions blow as smoke on the wind, and the struggle of fools ends bleakly. Yes, we do hear of a "food for final Hope" (Semichorus II of the Pities, After Scene), but "aerial music" accompanies it, and it is far removed from the spirit of Milton's specifically Christian resolution. Pessimism is at the core of Hardy's singularly strong-minded awareness of the impossibility of bringing intact Milton and the Miltonic dream to the modern world, a nihilism which negates three essential features of the Christian epic, God, Man ennobled with God's aid, and the possibility of Man's ascension to God. The repudiation of the epic tradition as exemplified by Milton's *Paradise Lost* is an act of a major poet in a major poem.

CHAPTER SIX

Hardy's Attitude Toward War

IN ONE OTHER WAY Hardy modified the epic: through his attitude toward the spectacle of human beings killing one another. The true epic, as E. M. W. Tillyard has pointed out, creates a "heroic impression"; it concerns "actions in which men know exactly what they are doing and rise through deliberate valour to a great height of resolution."[1] The artist, however, produces that effect more through his treatment, through the determined exercise of his will ("a great spirit," Tillyard says of the man who seeks to write an epic, "daring to risk everything on one great venture and knowing that in its execution he will be taxed to the limit of what a man can endure"), than through the subject matter.

We have already noted that Napoleon, fascinating as he was, did not excite Hardy's admiration. Like Walter Bagehot, Hardy thought of the Emperor as a man who walked wonderingly, as if he were amazed at being himself. Here was a mythmaker who, in a sense, perished before the inordinate demands of his own myth. He had abused the world's trust too ruthlessly and too often. George Bernard Shaw said of him that he believed mankind was "a troublesome pack of hounds only worth keeping for the sport of hunting with them," and Napoleon's cynicism, deepening with time, disgusted Hardy.

The temper of Hardy's treatment, therefore, is anti-heroic; but many passages in *The Dynasts* express a point of view that we have hardly considered as yet: the needlessness of war as a means of testing man's valor. It expresses a view that Hardy personally held. His opposition to war as a means of settling international disputes was well known; it underwent no significant change during his lifetime. He wrote a letter to *The Times*, published on June 28, 1904, admitting that Tolstoy's views were controversial, but added his commendation of "the blaze of glory that shines

86

from his masterly general indictment of war as a modern principle, with all its senseless and illogical crimes." He used whatever forum he could for the expression of this view: a reply to
W. T. Stead's request for a contribution to "A Crusade of Peace"
(1899); a letter to a professor at the University of Berlin who had
asked for a summing-up of his views on culture (1909), in the
course of which he denounced the "incubus of armaments, terri-
torial ambitions smugly disguised as patriotism, superstitions, conventions of every sort"; a petition protesting against the use of
"aerial vessels in war" (1911). He would gladly have agreed to
suppression of the play *An Englishman's Home* as "provocative,"
"since it gave Germany, even if pacific in intention beforehand, a
reason, or excuse, for directing her mind on a war with England."[2]

As a man of good will, he failed to foresee the possibility of
the Great War; like all his contemporaries, he could not believe
that any war of the future would kill so many, or prove so
catastrophic, as World War I. "The Sick Battle-God," a poem
written in 1901, exulted that the God of Battles "rarely gladdens
champions now," and spoke of Hardy's faith that sanity had replaced the madness of combat. "The Battle-god is god no more."
Hardy simply could not believe what the "music-hall Jingoes"
had been saying, that an open conflict between England and Germany was inevitable. In 1913 he wrote a lyric entitled "His
Country," in which he rejoiced that national boundaries were dis-
appearing; that men were becoming citizens of the world; that
no one could any longer desire "to weaken, crush, and blight."
He detested both Junkers and Jingoists, and hoped that some day
the sentiment of patriotism might be freed "from the narrow
meaning attached to it in the past."[3] Napoleon's wars had been
bad enough, so bloody that Hardy's imagination was unable to
conceive of anything worse while he accumulated the materials
for his epic-drama; the modern world had developed such wea-
pons, had become so "coldly scientific," that war was unthinkable.

He was, as a result of these views, unprepared for the German invasion of Belgium, or for what immediately developed thereafter, the horrifying destruction of England's best young men on the battlefields of France. Ended forever was his hope that men were becoming wise enough to outlaw war. As he looked at "the present infamous and disgraceful state of Europe—that most Christian Continent," he wondered what he, "an old man of seventy-four," might contribute to his nation's war effort. A poignant passage in *The Later Years* describes how, on September 2, 1914, many famous writers came together at Wellington House to consider the best means of presenting England's case to the populations of neutral countries. "Whatever the effects of the discussion," Hardy remembered, "the scene was impressive to more than one of them there . . . the yellow September sun shone in from the dusty street with a tragic cast upon them as they sat round the large blue table, full of misgivings, yet foreseeing in all their completeness the tremendous events that were to follow. The same evening Hardy left London—'the streets hot and sad, and bustling with soldiers and recruits'—to set about some contribution to the various forms of manifesto that had been discussed."[4] The lists of casualties expanded. When, on December 8, 1916, a précis of *The Dynasts* was read at a performance at Dorchester, Hardy contributed a note of highly personal feeling: "The contrast in point of humanity, honour and chivalry between our enemies in the present struggle, and those in the struggle with Napoleon a hundred years ago, does not show to the advantage of our modern methods of warfare and modern magnanimity. It is, indeed, no less than extraordinary that an additional centenary of civilization and moral effort have resulted in greater barbarities by far than any of those the much abused Bonaparte ever put in force against us. Heaven grant that all this scientific slaughter may soon cease, and that a sense of its folly will ensure its disappearance for ever."[5] It was a feeble hope, and the war which dragged on for another two years destroyed his wish that man might some day emerge from behind self-made bars, or that there might be "a fundamental ultimate Wisdom at the back of things."[6] To Professor Samuel C. Chew, among others, he confessed that "had he written *The Dynasts* after the Treaty of Versailles he could not have closed it upon a note of hope."[7] Probably the very last of his unpublished writings, dated December, 1927, was prepared for a French translation of *The Dynasts* by Yvonne Salmon; as a prefatory note, it commented on the "irresponsible governments" which dragged the people into warfare ("in which, even as in all war in general, human reason took little part"), and again predicted that "the *monist* theory of Cause and Effect" which he had adopted for artistic reasons in *The Dynasts* might some day prove to be "the true theory of the universe."[8]

Now it is striking that Hardy should want to transmit such doctrine through an epic-drama, a genre which often speaks of the noble relationship between arms and the man. Enough exists in the way of anti-war sentiment in *The Dynasts* to render suspect any easy judgment that Hardy's doctrine of Immanent Will dehumanizes or desensitizes his point of view. However mordant the speeches of the Spirits may be, Hardy's concern that "so sense-less-shaped a doing" must never happen again unifies the battle-scenes; gives point to the diplomatic negotiations; and makes meaningful the baffled, frustrated remarks of common people who cannot shape their own destinies. *The Dynasts* is one of the most effective denunciations of war in all English literature, and it is certainly Hardy's finest effort in this direction. Despite its imperfections, what Hardy referred to as "the hurried execution" of many of its pages, its conviction converts to eloquence the descriptions of strategy, and powerfully moves the reader to exclaim, along with the Spirit of the Pities, against "the ugly horror grossly regnant here" (III, I, v). It is true that Hardy overoptimistically assessed the willingness of men to renounce war as an instrument of national policy, now that the Napoleonic nightmare had ended; even in September, 1918, a decade after the completion of *The Dynasts*, he rejected the dark prophecies, contained in a circular letter sent to him, that the next war would be even more fiendish and horrible than the Great War which was still in progress.⁹ But he did not mistake or underestimate the waste inherent in any war. His anger at such waste runs as a noble undercurrent through all the acts of *The Dynasts*. He identifies himself not with the conquerors and the dynasts, whom he often enough derides, nor with the strategists and Parliamentarians who brilliantly gamble for the highest stakes, but with those who suffer, bleed, and all too often die before their time. In brief, *The Dynasts* was written to provide a history lesson, to become a mirror for magistrates wherein the meaning of the past might be reflected.

It is instructive to compare Hardy's treatment of war with the treatment accorded it in the most glorious of all epics, Homer's *Iliad*. I choose the *Iliad* rather than the *Odyssey* because the former is primarily a world of war, and because the peaceful interludes are briefly presented only for their relevance to the fighting which will break out again as soon as council-meetings or meals or sacrifices have ended; behind the funeral games of Patroclus looms the certainty of more combat on the windy plains of Troy. When Priam asks Achilles for eleven days of peace while Hector is being buried, he adds, "And on the twelfth we will do battle if need be." Nothing is more certain than that the twelfth day will be a day of war.

Homer's view of war is not a simple or unambiguous one. He describes war in all its savagery, its blood-madness, perhaps nowhere in more chilling detail than in the twenty-first book, in which Achilles kills young Trojan warriors in large numbers by the Xanthos River. The images of how men die are as graphic and explicit as anything Hardy records in *The Dynasts*. "For in the belly he smote him beside the navel, and all his bowels gushed out to the earth, and darkness covered his eyes as he lay gasping."

"But Achilles drew his sharp sword and smote on the collar-bone beside the neck, and all the two-edged sword sank into him, and he lay stretched prone upon the earth, and blood flowed dark from him and soaked the earth." Nevertheless, Homer's emphasis falls not upon the murdered but upon the murderer. We see Achilles, the "goodly," the "fleet-footed" and the "noble," the "spear-famed" and the "godlike," driven to superhuman deeds of revenge by his wrath, denying all pleas for mercy, implacable in his homicidal work, exulting in his strength and violence: "There slew he Thersilochos and Mydon and Astypyles and Mnesos and Thrasios and Ainios and Ophelestes. . . ." Achilles, fighting as a man possessed, is wantonly slaying; and finally the river itself rebels against his "might" and his "evil work." Choked with dead men, the deep-eddying stream can no longer flow out to the great sea, and in indignation it rises in tumultuous waves, so that the stream strikes violently against his shield and almost drowns him. ". . . And all the plain was filled with water-flood, and many beautiful arms and corpses of slain youths were drifting there." Only Hephaistos, by burning the dead and drying the raging flood, can save Achilles, and he intercedes only because Hera has asked him to do so.

War, in these terms, is a succession of horrors; the delight of killing stifles all impulse toward charity in the great Achilles, and the river wave must interrupt his frenzy ("for gods are mightier than men"); in turn, the action of the Xanthos must be checked by the action of other gods. The *Iliad* is tragic because, as Mark Van Doren rightly says, every answer must be wrong,[10] and because even the gods must war among themselves as they come to the realization that human life is far more complex than they had appreciated.

These things are true. But Homer, for all his perception of the waste of war and the pernicious effect it has upon the warrior, is unable to condemn it; and no reader of the *Iliad* can suppose, even for a moment, that Homer passes an over-all adverse judgment on the noble Achilles. Part of the sublimity of this epic lies in the fact that its creator has achieved an objective viewpoint, that he sees and understands everything, and that he refuses to take sides. War has its attractions too. More can be said. War is necessary for the testing of manly virtue; it is the highest test. Werner Jaeger, in his monumental study *Paideia: The Ideals of Greek Culture*, has demonstrated clearly the relationship between the older concept of *arete* as warlike prowess and the newer concept, expressed by Phoinix, the teacher of Achilles, that one must be both a speaker of words and a doer of deeds.[11] One must be—in short—a hero, and prove his heroic stature by winning the first prize in whatever he undertakes; nowhere may this proof be considered more unchallengeable than on the battlefield. Yet intellectual sovereignty is prized too, and its possession an evidence of true nobility. Achilles, hero of the *Iliad*, is closer to the older concept; Odysseus, hero of the *Odyssey*, a "cunning" man, is obviously closer to the ideal promulgated by Phoinix.

In the *Iliad*, however, the tension between the two ideals expresses itself as an ambivalent attitude toward war. There is no better way to study this ambivalence than to look more closely at the description of the shield of Achilles, given in full detail in Book XVIII. Hephaistos, the lame god, fashions therein "two fair cities of mortal men." One depicts a world of peace: "espousals and marriage feasts . . . young men . . . whirling in the dance . . . the women standing each at her door." In the assembly-place judgment is being passed on the blood-price of a slain man. The other depicts a world at war: "two armies in siege with glittering arms." The besieged are determined not to yield. "On the wall there stood to guard it their dear wives and infant children, and with these the old men; but the rest went forth, and their leaders were Ares and Pallas Athene, both wrought in gold, and golden was the vesture they had on. Goodly and great were they in their armour, even as gods, far seen around, and the people at their feet were smaller." It is the miracle of Homer that these two cities, representing two ways of life, are depicted as equally attractive, and that the reasons for their attractiveness should be given fairly. For Homer knew that, delightful as are the teeming vineyard and the dancing-place, so too are the glittering bronze of armor, the "corslet brighter than a flame of fire," the "massive helmet," the chance to prove oneself a hero and to earn great honor among one's peers.

The "wasting wars" of the Napoleonic era provoke the Spirit Sinister to muse, "My argument is that War makes rattling good history; but Peace is poor reading" (I, II, v). Hardy has taken the measure of war, and come to harsh conclusions about the irresponsibility of sovereigns. *The Dynasts* praises only a few things in this sorry world of exploited peoples: the poetry inherent in man's existence, as when the Spirit of the Pities describes the action on the road near Astorga, Spain (II, III, i); Pitt, reminding England of its vocation and duty; the resoluteness of a character like Queen Louisa of Prussia (II, I, viii); the loyalty of Marshal Ney, "that matchless chief" (III, VII, iv); and, in one remarkable passage, the sight of troopers.

> Accoutred in kaleidoscopic hues
> That would persuade us war has beauty in it. . . .[12]

Hardy knew well enough the nature of the fatal attraction that war has for its combatants. But he did not dwell on it. Rather, his descriptions emphasize, in battle after battle, the coarsening of human character as the deaths accumulate. At Austerlitz, for example, the most horrifying moment comes when Dokhtorof's column, consisting of two thousand men, finds itself trapped on the ice of the Satschan lake. The Emperor, watching the scene "with a vulpine smile," orders a nearby battery to direct its fire at the ice over which the Austrians are crossing. The despairing groans of the dying reach the ears of the watchers (Napoleon among them) "like ironical huzzas" (I, VI, iv). In one striking scene (II, III, i), Hardy describes a Spanish cellar, covered by "heaps of damp straw, in which ragged figures are lying half-buried, many of the men in the uniform of English line-regiments, and the women and children in clouts of all descriptions, some being nearly naked." These deserters and prostitutes no longer care how the war progresses, and when an officer threatens to shoot them, they cry, "You may shoot us, captain, or the French may shoot us, or the devil may take us; we don't care which!" Napoleon, for the crossing of the Danube at Wagram (II, IV, ii), must force his troops to move ahead; he has "the restlessness of a wild animal," is "plastered with mud, and dribbling with rain-water," and bears "no resemblance to anything dignified or official."

Homer, who gave in dense detail the pedigree and worth of his warriors even as they fell, so that each man's life became a separate, distinct tragedy in the *Iliad*, would not have understood Hardy's emphasis on the facelessness of battle; yet this anonymity of modern warfare is part of Hardy's epic design, and if there are no heroes, there is at any rate a multitude of victims. At the field of Jena, Hardy's Dumb Show reveals a world in fog, soldiers encountering each other almost by accident, a confused melée. The regiments "crash like trees at felling time" (II, I, iv). The battle between Junot and Wellesley in the hills of Portugal rages: "a dust is raised by this ado," writes Hardy, using the passive-voice construction to good effect, "and moans of men and shrieks of horses are heard. Close by the carnage the little Meceira stream continues to trickle unconcernedly to the sea" (II, II, vii). The Field of Talavera is a hot, confused graveyard (II, IV, iv). Albuera is a chaos of "smoke, steel, sweat, curses, and blood." Soldiers discharge muskets in each other's faces. "Hot corpses, their mouths blackened by cartridge-biting, and surrounded by cast-away knapsacks, firelocks, hats, stocks, flint-boxes, and priming-horns, together with red and blue rags of clothing, gaiters, epaulettes, limbs, and viscera, accumulate on the slopes, increasing from twos and threes to half-dozens, and from half-dozens to heaps, which steam with their own warmth as the spring rain falls gently upon them." It is a "slaughtery," and the hacked bones of the dead lie on the grieving earth.

> What man can grieve? what woman weep?
> Better than waking is to sleep! Albuera! (II, VI, iv)

Yet even Albuera is prologue to greater madness: the march to Moscow and the long retreat back to France. Borodino, with its fumes of nitre and the reek of gore, is "wholesale butchery," in which horses are "maimed in myriads," boys call on their mothers, and veterans blaspheme God and man (III, I, v). The conflagration of the Russian capital is fittingly bitter conclusion to Napoleon's investiture. "Large pieces of canvas aflare sail away on the gale like balloons. Cocks crow, thinking it sunrise, ere they are burnt to death" (III, I, vii). As Moscow "vanishes away," the march to the west becomes the ghastliest of all realities. A "dun-piled caterpillar" shuffles its length "in painful heaves along." The soldiers must return along the "confused expanse" of the road from Smolensk into Lithuania, to Borodino and the "unburied horrors beyond name" (III, I, ix). The snows of winter began to fall. "The marching figures drop rapidly, and almost immediately become white gravemounds." The landscape, bleak and blasted, waits: "Nature is mute. Save for the incessant flogging of the wind-broken and lacerated horses there are no sounds."

Of the horrors of the Bridge of the Beresina at Studzianka, Hardy can speak only with shocked amazement. Round shot and canister pour into the midst of the fugitives. When the bridge crumbles, thousands drown, including mothers and their children. Hardy did not have to invent these "stricken shades in a limbo of gloom" who "cut rashers from a dead horse, and grill them in the flames, using gunpowder for salt to eat them with," and who gradually become insane and die on the frozen steppes of unforgiving Russia. "The flames of the burning bridge go out as it consumes to the water's edge, and darkness mantles all, nothing continuing, but the purl of the river and the clickings of floating ice" (III, I, xi).

It is all downhill now, and the conclusion of the Peninsular War seems anticlimactic, though its "indescribable tumult," the deaths of countless civilians in a "billowy throng," and the raids of "cloaked creatures of the starlight" upon the wounded after the main current of the battle has ebbed are appalling enough. On the plain of Vitoria "a Noah's-ark of living creatures in one vast procession" carry the loot of plunder, and Wellington allows his men, who have "striven long and gallantly," to do what they want (III, II, iii).

At Leipzig Napoleon's soldiers fall "like sedge before the scythe," "and bayonets slant and reek" (III, III, iii). At the field of Ligny the monster Devastation rises in one of Hardy's few Biblical-shaped passages (III, VI, v). Then follows the fight without quarter, in which bayonets are unfixed and musket-butts are used to brain the enemy. The French grapeshot notches the soldiers of Brunswick, and "the Dynasts' gory gear" moves toward its last piteous moments. On the road to Waterloo, at the village of Genappe, the stormy weather oppresses the locked combatants:

—Cannon upon the foul and flooded road,
Cavalry in the cornfields mire-bestrowed,
With frothy horses floundering to their knees. . . . (III, VI, viii)

The fields are sodden with rain and churned mud, and the firing of the English batteries creates a concussion that shakes the hill itself. "Hard pounding this, my men," says Wellington. The smoke becomes so thick that "the position of the battalions is revealed only by the flashing of the priming-pans and muzzles, and by the furious oaths heard behind the cloud" (III, VII, vii). It has become a battle of "wounds, smoke, the fumes of gunpowder, and the steam from the hot viscera of grape-torn horses and men." Sixty cannon smash into the Old Guard, and as they retreat, the dead define their track. The clocks of the world strike the last empery-hour. It is a slaughter, an Esdraelon, so frightful that we are not surprised when Hardy informs us that some of the fleeing French soldiers "blow out their own brains as they fly." The massacre continues when the remnants of the Old Guard refuse to surrender to Colonel Hugh Halkett; their laughter is hollow, "as from people in hell." Hardy summarizes the battle—all battles in the mechanized insanity that passes for warfare—before he turns to Napoleon's spectral questionings in the wood of Bossu:

> The reds disappear from the sky, and the dusk grows deeper. The action of the battle degenerates to a hunt, and recedes further and further into the distance southwards. When the tramplings and shouts of the combatants have dwindled, the lower sounds are noticeable that come from the wounded: hopeless appeals, cries for water, elaborate blasphemies, and impotent execrations of Heaven and hell. In the vast and dusky shambles black slouching shapes begin to move, the plunderers of the dead and dying.

> The night grows clear and beautiful, and the moon shines musingly down. But instead of the sweet smell of green herbs and dewy rye as at her last beaming upon these fields, there is now the stench of gunpowder and a muddy stew of crushed crops and gore (III, I, v).

Modern war, in *The Dynasts*, is unnecessary for the advancement of nations or the happiness of peoples. It is stupid as well, because there are no victories great enough to compensate for the "loam and blood" exacted as the necessary price, and the defeats are often near-things. (Napoleon, exulting during Ney's assault on La Haye Saint, thought that he might sleep in Brussels that evening, and Wellington, upset by his teetering position, swore "by every God that war can call upon" to defend his position.) It affords no time for the kind of question Diomedes asks Glaukos upon the Trojan plains, "Who are thou, noble sir, of mortal men?

For never have I beheld thee in glorious battle ere this, yet now hast thou far outstripped all men in thy hardihood, seeing thou abidest my far-shadowing spear. Luckless are the fathers whose children face my sight. But if thou art some immortal come down from heaven, then will not I fight with heavenly gods." Or for the kind of answer that the son of Hippolochos provides: "Great-hearted Tydeides, why enquirest thou of my generation? Even as are the generations of leaves such are those likewise of men; the leaves that be the wind scattereth on the earth, and the forest buddeth and putteth forth more again, when the season of spring is at hand; so of the generations of men one putteth forth and another ceaseth. Yet if thou wilt, have thine answer, that thou mayest well know our lineage, whereof many men have knowledge. There is a city Ephyre in the heart of Argos. . . ." The enemies kill each other blindly, anonymously; they do not know each other, or wish to know each other, personally; under other circumstances, they would not be enemies at all. Such, certainly, is the meaning of that poignant scene at the Alberche brook, where the English and the French shamefacedly drink together "in homely need," grasp hands across it, and seal "their sameness as earth's sojourners" (II, IV, v). Perhaps worst of all, modern war is bestial and dehumanizing. Singularly missing from Hardy's chronicle of wars is the occasional generous gesture of a Homeric hero, the movement made by an unpredictable magnanimous conqueror to ease the lot of the defeated, the dying, the betrayed; not because Hardy was unaware that such gestures might be made even in the heart of the inferno, but because his concept of war sternly repudiated sentiment, and because for him, as for Thomas Campbell, far too many thousands of human beings had died that Caesar might be great. The very word "great" has a bitter flavor in an epic-drama that distrusts the pretensions of dynasts. If the Duke of Wellington was correct in saying (as he is reported to have said) that a "great" country can have no such thing as a little war, the nations of the world, determined to demonstrate their importance, will bring on more Waterloos. It is a fearsome moral. We can only sympathize with Hardy's belief that war had become obsolete in the first decade of the twentieth century.

CHAPTER SEVEN

Conclusion

THE EPIC-DRAMA having been published, Hardy did not again attempt the writing of a long poem. His books of poetry are made up of short lyrical, meditative, satirical, and experimental pieces; no single piece exceeds more than a few hundred lines, and a reader might well be surprised at the variety of themes and techniques in his more than eight hundred *Collected Poems.* Hardy's apparent determination to avoid long narrative in any form left him ample time to concentrate on the kind of creative writing he loved best. His books after *The Well-Beloved* (1897) may be listed as follows: *Wessex Poems* (1898); *Poems of the Past and the Present* (1902); an edition of selected poems of William Barnes (1908); *Time's Laughingstocks and Other Verses* (1909); a collection of previously uncollected tales, published in various nineteenth-century periodicals, *A Changed Man and Other Tales* (1913); *Satires of Circumstance* (1914); *Selected Poems* (1916); *Moments of Vision* (1917); *Late Lyrics and Earlier* (1922); *The Famous Tragedy of the Queen of Cornwall* (1923); *Human Shows* (1925); *Winter Words* (1928); various individual lyrics, subsequently incorporated in reprintings of other collections; and, of course, the two volumes of his autobiography.

Hardy was not completely satisfied with *The Dynasts,* and he knew well that it suffered from imperfections. The disapproval in the reviews of Part First stemmed (Hardy thought) from *odium theologicum* rather than from the unfinished condition of the poem; but the attacks almost led him to give up the writing of the subsequent volumes. "It is most unlikely that I shall carry the drama any further," he wrote to Edmund Gosse on January 17, 1904; and when Gosse reproved him, he wrote again, on January 31, to say that he had been appalled by some of his oversights in Part First. "I had meant to keep it by me longer, but a sudden feeling last autumn that I should never finish it, and that I would get rid of what was done, caused me to rush it out incontinently." Gosse, he knew, would piece out his imperfections with his thoughts.[1] Later (February 28, 1906) Hardy wrote to Gosse that he might revise "some of the less carefully considered [passages] in a future edition" (he did not get around to it). When the final volumes of *The Dynasts* had appeared, he shrugged in frustration. It had proved impossible to hold on to the manuscript, carefully reworking it until all "hasty lines and pages" had been reworked. But he had no more to add in the way of a Fourth Part. To an inquiry made in 1914 as to whether he might continue his analysis of *The Dynasts* into the current century, he answered that other pens than his would have to take up the assignment.[2]

He read with close attention the reviews that greeted the appearance of the different parts of *The Dynasts*. He did not care for them, partly because they rebuked him for having abandoned the novel, and because they advanced the opinion (still held by some admirers of Hardy's novels) that the dialogue of *The Dynasts* was "the prose of the novelist cut into lengths." They worried over how it should be classified: "Thomas Hardy's Latest Production—Magnum Opus or Monstrosity?" Some wondered whether Hardy was perpetrating a joke on his public. A few protested their inability to judge the work, and preferred to leave the final decision to a generation still unborn, or to a race of giants that might some day come into existence.[3]

More than anything else, however, Hardy detested the way in which his views on existence and the nature of the universe had been misinterpreted and vulgarized. In a private memorandum after the publication of Part First, he wrote, "The very fact of my having tried to spread over art the latest illumination of the time has darkened counsel in respect of me." Nor could numerous enthusiastic private letters lighten his strong reaction against what he considered to be, in essence, a patronizing claptrap; the articles of praise which began to appear after the completion of his trilogy, and which often admitted the critic's desire to make amends for a hostile or uncomprehending review of Hardy's intentions in Part First, were appreciated, but could not completely undo the damage.

Hardy had emphasized that *The Dynasts* was intended "simply for mental performance, and not for the stage." Nevertheless, abridged versions were prepared and produced: one by Harley Granville-Barker that ran at the Kingsway Theatre for seventy-two performances in 1914-15, and that enjoyed a revival by the Oxford University Dramatic Society in 1920[4]; and another, made up of Wessex scenes, that Hardy himself selected, by the Dorchester Debating and Dramatic Society in 1908, and again in 1916. Granville-Barker's production at the Kingsway was particularly impressive, and Rebecca West, after listing her reservations about the way in which the theatre had compromised Hardy's epic-drama, wrote that she had just seen "one of the greatest plays that have been on the English stage. . . . It was unquestionably great and marvellously beautiful."[5] Many years later the British Broadcasting Corporation used selections that excited the imaginations of thousands of listeners.

There is evidence to support the view that Hardy, who had been preparing for the writing of *The Dynasts* much of his life, took pride in it as the greatest of all his literary achievements. The writer for the *Daily News* who telephoned him on August 28, 1914, to tell him that "everybody seems to be reading *The Dynasts* just now," was commenting on the timeliness of the epic-drama during years of crisis (and Hardy's treatment of the Napoleonic madness was to become fashionable again during World War II). Hardy was appreciative of A. D. Godley's "felicitous" reference to *The Dynasts* on the occasion when Oxford awarded him the honorary degree of Doctor of Letters: *"opus eius tam scriptoris facundia quam rerum quae tractantur magnitudine*

102

insignitum." And, in the poignant chapter entitled "Some Fare-wells" in *The Later Years*, Hardy noted that an address sent to him by St. John Ervine and signed by 106 younger writers con-cluded with the sentences, "From your first book to your last you have written in the 'high style, as when that men to kinges write,' and you have crowned a great prose with a noble poetry. We thank you, Sir, for all that you have written . . . but most of all, perhaps, for *The Dynasts*."[6]

Hardy did not approve of biography as a substitute for criti-cism, and once, after having looked through Colvin's *Keats* still another time before returning it to Sydney C. Cockerell, he wrote somberly that "a poet may be much injured by over-criti-cism . . . too much commenting and prying into motives etc., rub the bloom off the poetry."[7] But perhaps there has not been enough judicious commenting on Hardy's motives for writing *The Dynasts*. Because the early reviews disparaged the work, or confessed to puzzlement, Hardy admitted that he had not made himself understood despite his most earnest efforts. His work described events of some magnitude, as Godley had said, and was itself a large statement. By following the example of Milton's *Paradise Lost*, he anticipated, and tried to minimize, the tedium that many readers experience in the presence of a long poem; and his list of "books read or pieces looked at" for 1887, the same year in which he was so struck by Addison's description of Mil-ton's art, included not only Milton but Homer ("Chapman's *Iliad*, Lord Derby's ditto, Worsley's *Odyssey*"), Virgil, Dante, *The Cid*, *Lay of the Nibelungen*, Goethe, and *Don Quixote*.[8] He was, to say the least, familiar with epics, and he always thought of the subject-matter of *The Dynasts* as epic in scope, and worthy of the high seriousness that has marked the great epics of the past. Also, by limiting his time period from the moment of Na-poleon's maximum splendor and arrogance (the crowning of Milan) to the moment of the Emperor's recognition that Water-loo ended forever his dynastic ambitions, Hardy planned to control and unify the events of a crowded decade. And his choice of the Immanent Will as poetic metaphor for "the First or Fundamental Energy" was *choric* in Tillyard's sense, in that it expressed the feelings of a large number of his contemporaries. (An epic does not have to be primarily patriotic, although *The Dynasts* is that too.)

Not all artists approach the meridian of their powers with so powerful a theme waiting, largely complete in its outline, for execution. It was, as Hardy said, an "independent plunge" because of his resolve to say forthrightly what he had never said before. He brought to his writing an emotional intensity that renders incredible any statement to the effect that as a "stage manager" he is cool, detached, and objectively ironic. His horror at all that war implies shapes the selection of materials to an uncanny degree. The "shipped battalions" who cross the English Channel "like sheep a-pen" come reluctantly, and many years are to pass, untold lives are to end, before Napoleon's career is to be interrupted by a final shattering military defeat. The thrills which we may feel at the splendid sight of massed lines of handsome soldiers, of national purpose made palpable, of ceremony and exalted ritual, do not compensate for these "unwonted spectacles of sweat and scare," the "piteous shrieks and calls" rising from "the pale mob," that inevitably follow. Whatever glory war offers on the parade-ground disappears on the battlefield. In the words of C. Lewis Hind, Hardy's poetry is "pregnant with pity for humanity."[9]

Hardy, as T. S. Eliot remarked, apprehended his matter as a poet and an artist.[10] *The Dynasts* is so firmly linked with the traditions of epic poetry, it so honestly acknowledges them even when saying they will not work for an "older, more invidious, more nervous, more quizzical" world, that a recent critic's description of it as one of "the great eccentric works of our time" seems eccentric in itself.[11] *The Dynasts* is not to be arrayed with James Joyce's *Ulysses*, with Ezra Pound's *The Cantos*, or with

T. S. Eliot's *The Waste Land*. Its heritage is Homer, Virgil, Milton; and even though Hardy declared in his Preface that its literary form had been "shaped with a single view to the modern expression of a modern outlook," he could not repudiate so easily a lifetime of reading and literary preference.

As part of his achievement he gave us his depiction of Napoleon as a figure who, for all his faults, deserved his moment of history. It is a remarkable portrait, and only one of many. There is more to say about the disturbing personal tragedies of a host of figures whom Napoleon victimizes; whose ambitions unrealized and happiness denied intensify the meaning of Hardy's epic-drama. Hardy admired Josephine as a woman who never wished Napoleon ill, and who, cast aside and dying, still loved him. He detested Marie Louise, an unfeeling, unloyal wretch who married for policy and became a whining and childlike creature of the court in her old age.[12] He paid his respects to Queen Louisa of Prussia, who pored "on musty chronicles" and mused

> on usurpations long forgot,
> And other historied dramas of high wrong. (III, I, viii)

And in countless vivid scenes he brings before us Villeneuve, Admiral Decrès, Alexander, Napoleon's marshals and Napoleon's men, earnestly trying to believe in the rightness of their Emperor's every decision, and determined to remain true to the very moment that the musket ball annihilates them.

It is a magnificent cavalcade, and it could easily have escaped Hardy's control. What Hardy wrote to Sir Henry Newbolt on January 11, 1905, was true: he had been obliged to condense so strictly that he could not give a twentieth part of the detail he should have liked to give.[13] The artistic control which unifies this host of characters, these diverse actions, and this sanguinary decade is always firm, and never less than equal to the heavy responsibility Hardy imposed upon himself. For a full fifteen years it absorbed his creative energies. He planned it elaborately. He wrote it with a conviction that no other theory of modern philosophy explained so well the structure of the universe. The modern world, too, hears

> sounds of insult, shame, and wrong,
> And trumpets blown for wars,

and Hardy's epigraph, like the work it prefaces, continues to echo resonantly in the minds of all its readers.

Notes

CHAPTER ONE

1. Frederic William Maitland, *The Life and Letters of Leslie Stephen* (New York, 1906), p. 274.

2. *Ibid.*, pp. 276-277.

3. John Paterson, *The Making of* The Return of the Native, University of California *English Studies*, XIX (Berkeley, 1960), 6. (Cf. Carl J. Weber's bibliographical study, "Hardy's Grim Note in *The Return of the Native*," *The Papers of the Bibliographical Society of America*, XXXVI [1942], 37-45.)

4. Paterson, p. 89.

5. For a brief but interesting account of these reviews, see Edmund Blunden's *Thomas Hardy* (London, 1958), pp. 42-46.

6. Richard Little Purdy, *Thomas Hardy: A Bibliographical Study* (London, 1954), pp. 36-40.

7. Florence Emily Hardy, *The Early Life of Thomas Hardy, 1840-1891* (New York, 1928), p. 188. This, and its companion volume, *The Later Years of Thomas Hardy, 1892-1928* (New York, 1930), were dictated by Hardy to his wife.

8. Purdy, p. 44.

9. In a letter written to the *St. James's Gazette*, January 19, 1883, p. 14.

10. *Early Life*, p. 235.

11. Ernest Brennecke, Jr., *The Life of Thomas Hardy* (New York, 1925), p. 9.

12. Carl J. Weber, *Hardy and the Lady from Madison Square* (Waterville, Maine, 1952), pp. 65-66.

13. *Early Life*, p. 291. Hardy does not go into any detail about the earlier rejections of the manuscript.

14. *Ibid.*

15. *Ibid.*, pp. 272-273.

16. I find rather appealing the explanation of Hardy's "accommodation" that Carl J. Weber provides in his biography, *Hardy of Wessex* (Hamden, Connecticut, 1962), pp. 146-147: "Hardy was as much amused by London editors as by Dorset rustics. John Durbeyfield walking with a bias in his gait was no funnier than Editor Locker prodded and goaded by his board of directors on the road of propriety."

17. *Later Years*, p. 37. (Cf. Mary Ellen Chase, *Thomas Hardy from Serial to Novel* [Minneapolis, 1927], pp. 115-177.)

18. Robert C. Slack, "The Text of Hardy's *Jude the Obscure*," *Nineteenth-Century Fiction*, XI (March, 1957), 261-275.

19. Carl J. Weber edited the text for Harper's Modern Classics (1957).

20. *Later Years*, pp. 50-52.

21. *Ibid.*, p. 65.

22. The fact that Hardy did not date all his poems, and kept printing compositions from his early years in volumes of poetry published during his later years, has created something of a bibliographical problem for Hardy scholars, particularly those interested in tracing the development of Hardy's ideas.

23. *Early Life*, p. 131.

24. Weber, *Hardy of Wessex*, p. 38.

25. *Early Life*, p. 135.

26. *Ibid.*, p. 64.

27. *Later Years*, pp. 57-58.

CHAPTER TWO

1. Evelyn Hardy (ed.), *Thomas Hardy's Notebooks* (London, 1955), p. 32.

2. *Early Life*, p. 66.

3. F. W. Maitland, p. 264.

4. Helen Garwood, *Thomas Hardy: An Illustration of the Philosophy of Schopenhauer* (Philadelphia, 1911), p. 11.

5. Carl J. Weber, *Hardy of Wessex*, p. 203.

6. Carl J. Weber, "Hardy's Copy of Schopenhauer," *Colby Library Quarterly*, IV (November, 1957), 217-224.

7. See William R. Rutland, *Thomas Hardy: A Study of His Writings and Their Background* (Oxford, 1938), pp. 68-70, for a strong statement on this matter. Rutland rules out the possibility of pure coincidence in the resemblance of ideas between Mill and Hardy.

8. J. O. Bailey, *Thomas Hardy and the Cosmic Mind: A New Reading of The Dynasts* (Chapel Hill, North Carolina, 1956), p. 11. Hardy knew that his views on meliorism differed from those of Schopenhauer, and said as much in his "Apology," prefixed to *Late Lyrics and Earlier* (1922). See *Collected Poems* (New York, 1958), p. 532.

9. Hardy's phrase, quoted by William Archer in "Real Conversations. Conversation 1.—With Mr. Thomas Hardy," *The Critic*, XXXVIII (April, 1901), 316. The scholar referred to in the text is J. O. Bailey. Professor Bailey's book has been challenged by T. R. Dale, who wrote that "Hardy's presentation of an unconscious will gradually becoming conscious is . . . directly and essentially opposed to Von Hartmann's teaching." *Notes and Queries*, CCVI (March, 1961), 100-101.

10. Hardy, *loc. cit.*

11. Bailey, p. 27.

12. *Times Literary Supplement,* February 19, 1904, p. 53.

13. *Later Years*, p. 125.

14. *Ibid.*, p. 217.

15. *Early Life*, p. 214.
16. *Later Years*, p. 73.
17. *Ibid.*, p. 226.
18. *Ibid.*, p. 219.
19. *Ibid.*, p. 128.
20. *Early Life*, p. 293.
21. *Later Years*, p. 121.
22. *Ibid.*, p. 210.
23. *Collected Poems*, p. 526.
24. *Early Life*, p. 286.
25. *Ibid.*, pp. 63-64.
26. *Ibid.*, p. 210.
27. *Later Years*, p. 176.
28. *Ibid.*, pp. 13-14.
29. *Early Life*, p. 111.
30. *Later Years*, p. 7.
31. *Ibid.*, p. 49.
32. *Ibid.*, p. 183.
33. Thomas Hardy, *Tess of the d'Urbervilles: A Pure Woman*, Library Edition (London, 1958), p. 324.
34. *Ibid.*, p. 456.
35. Thomas Hardy, *Jude the Obscure*, Library Edition (London, 1958), p. vi.
36. *Collected Poems*, p. 3.
37. *Ibid.*, p. 529.

Chapter Three

1. Evelyn Hardy, *Thomas Hardy's Notebooks and Some Letters from Julia Augusta Martin* (London, 1955), pp. 45-46.
2. *Early Life*, p. 140.
3. Hardy uses the phrase in *The Dynasts*, I, II, v, but he did not invent it.
4. *Early Life*, p. 168.
5. *Later Years*, p. 57.
6. Hardy's footnote to III, VI, ii, of *The Dynasts* has often been quoted to indicate the lengths to which Hardy would go to corroborate his facts: "This famous ball has become so embedded in this history of the Hundred Days as to be an integral part of it. Yet in spite of the efforts that have been made to locate the room which saw the memorable gathering (by the present writer more than thirty years back, among other enthusiasts), a dispassionate judgment must deny that its site has as yet been proven. Even Sir W. Fraser is not convincing. The event happened less than a century ago, but the spot is almost as phantasmal in its elusive mystery as towered

Camelot, the palace of Priam, or the hill of Calvary." I interpret this note to mean that Hardy was relieved the ballroom had not been discovered; because it resisted the prying of historians, it retained forever its charm as an unsolved mystery. When Rebekah Owen sent to Hardy a clipping from an English newspaper which claimed to identify the exact site of the ball, Hardy answered her, on December 6, 1907, with the comment that he remained unconvinced. He preferred that the site of the room should remain unknown, "as it helps the romance of the event—unless, indeed, it could be where Byron puts it—at the Hotel de Ville, the only place worthy of the occasion." There the poet speaks. (Quoted by Carl J. Weber, ed., *The Letters of Thomas Hardy* [Waterville, Maine, 1954], pp. 73-74.)

7. Emma Clifford, " 'The Trumpet-Major Notebook' and *The Dynasts*," *Review of English Studies*, VIII (May, 1957), 149-161.

8. William R. Rutland, *Thomas Hardy: A Study of His Writings and Their Background* (Oxford, 1938), pp. 291-317. See also Weber, *Hardy of Wessex*, pp. 276-277, for a partial listing of the English and French books about the Napoleonic period in Hardy's personal library; also *Later Years*, p. 275, where Hardy writes to Edward Clodd on New Year's Eve, 1907, "...I have been living in Wellington's campaigns so much lately that, like George IV, I am almost positive that I took part in the battle of Waterloo, and have written of it from memory."

9. Carroll A. Wilson, *A Descriptive Catalogue of the Grolier Club Centenary Exhibition, 1940, of the Works of Thomas Hardy, O.M.*, Colby College Monograph No. 9 (1940), p. 47.

10. *Early Life*, p. 150.

11. *Later Years*, p. 226.

12. *Ibid.*, pp. 226-227.

13. *Early Life*, p. 188.

14. *Ibid.*, pp. 219-220.

15. *Ibid.*, p. 266.

16. Ruth A. Firor, *Folkways in Thomas Hardy* (Philadelphia, 1931), p. 301.

17. Wilson. p. 7.

18. Elizabeth Cox Wright, *Metaphor, Sound, and Meaning in Bridges' The Testament of Beauty* (Philadelphia, 1951), p. 16.

19. *Early Life*, p. 290.

20. Hoxie N. Fairchild, "The Immediate Source of *The Dynasts*," *PMLA*, LXVII (March, 1952), 43-64.

21. John Bailey, writing for the Napoleon Centenary Supplement issued by *The Times* in 1921, has said that *The Dynasts* was one of the two greatest appearances of Napoleon in English poetry (the other being in the second of Meredith's four *Odes in Contribution to the Song of French History*). Bailey is puzzled by the failure of the Romantic poets to do

much with the Napoleonic theme, and by the failure of the Victorian poets to do anything with it, since "poetry can never have said her last word" of such a man. The essay is reprinted under the title "Napoleon in Poetry" in *The Continuity of Letters* (Oxford, 1923), pp. 218-241.

22. *Early Life*, p. 306.

23. *Later Years*, p. 9.

Chapter Four

1. Weber, *Hardy and the Lady from Madison Square*, p. 89.

2. S. F. Johnson, "Burke and Hardy," *T.L.S.*, December 7, 1956, p. 731. Johnson also notes Hardy's indebtedness to Book II, x, for his view of the importance of illusion in art. Burke has written, "No work of art can be great, but as it deceives; to be otherwise is the prerogative of nature only." Hardy restates this opinion in several places.

3. "There is no reason to doubt Burke's direct influence. Nor is there any doubt that Burke's *Enquiry* made its finest contribution to imaginative literature through the stimulus it gave Thomas Hardy."—J. T. Boulton, ed., *A Philosophical Enquiry into the Origin of our Ideas of the Sublime and Beautiful*, by Edmund Burke (London, 1958), p. cxx. The standard history of the concept of the sublime in the eighteenth century, which relates the *Equiry* to the writings of Burke's contemporaries, is Samuel H. Monk's *The Sublime* (Ann Arbor, Michigan, 1960).

4. *Burke*, p. 68.

5. *Ibid.*, p. 72.

6. Clifford, pp. 157-158.

7. *T.L.S.*, February 5, 1904, p. 37.

8. Thomas Hardy, "Fine Passages in Verse and Prose: Selected by Living Men of Letters," *Fortnightly Review*, XLII (August, 1887), 304.

9. Thomas Hardy, "The Profitable Reading of Fiction," *Forum*, V (March, 1888), 68.

10. Thomas Hardy, "Candour in English Fiction," *New Review*, II (January, 1890), 16.

11. Thomas Hardy, "The Science of Fiction," *New Review*, IV (April, 1891), 318.

12. Statistics have only a limited usefulness for this kind of study; but Elizabeth Cathcart Hickson has estimated that only 1,470 lines of the 10,553 total are in prose and the total does not include stage directions and dumb-shows. *The Versification of Thomas Hardy* (Philadelphia, 1931), *passim*.

13. Cf. I, VI, i and I, VI, v.

14. F. L. Lucas, *Tragedy: Serious Drama in Relation to Aristotle's Poetics* (London, 1957), *passim*.

15. Rutland, p. 291.

CHAPTER FIVE

1. Charles E. Whitmore, "Mr. Hardy's *Dynasts* as Tragic Drama," *MLN*, XXXIX (December, 1924), 455-460.

2. Bailey, pp. 33-86. Bailey's analysis of the role that each Spirit plays is careful and sensible. Only minor points seem debatable. For example, Hardy's view that the Spirit of the Years "approximates to the passionless Insight of the Ages" does not seem to justify Bailey's characterization of the Spirit as calmly compassionate.

3. It would be fascinating, but distracting from the subject-matter of the present chapter, to show this in rich detail. An important study which carefully differentiates among various kinds of irony as understood and used by writers of the Renaissance is Norman Knox's *The Word "Irony" and Its Context, 1500-1755* (Durham, North Carolina, 1961).

4. Bailey, p. 69.

CHAPTER SIX

1. E. M. W. Tillyard, *The English Epic and Its Background* (London, 1954), pp. 10-11.

2. *Later Years*, p. 162.

3. *Ibid.*, p. 174.

4. *Ibid.*, p. 163.

5. *The Times* (December 9, 1916), p. 11.

6. *Later Years*, pp. 165-166.

7. For Chew's comment see *A Literary History of England*, ed. Albert C. Baugh (New York, 1948), p. 1470.

8. John G. Rideout, "Hardy's Last Words on *The Dynasts*," *Colby Mercury*, VI (June 2, 1936), 85-87. For the French version, see *La Revue Nouvelle* (Paris, Jan.-Feb., 1928), pp. 40-41.

9. *Later Years*, pp. 189-190.

10. Mark Van Doren, *On Great Poems of Western Literature* (New York, 1962), p. 36.

11. Werner Jaeger, *Paideia: The Ideals of Greek Culture*, trans. Gilbert Highet (New York, 1945), I, 3-8.

12. Hardy, at the Queen's birthday review of 1893, was impressed by the "superb accoutrements" which transformed the Aides into warriors, and spoke of the parade as "a romantic scene, pathetically gay, especially as to the horses in the gallop past." *Later Years*, p. 19. This event may have been the inspiration, more than a decade later, of the Spirit of the Pities' description of handsome cavalry troops in III, VII, iv.

CHAPTER SEVEN

1. Wilson, p. 47.

2. *Ibid.*, p. 48.

3. For a full listing of such reviews, see Carl J. Weber's *The First Hundred Years of Hardy, 1840-1940: A Centenary Bibliography of Hardiana* (Waterville, Maine, 1942). Representative reviews are printed in the *Academy*, LXVI (January 23, 1904), 95; the *Athenaeum*, No. 3978 (January 23, 1904), 123; *Atlantic Monthly*, XCIII (May, 1904), 713; *Current Literature*, XI (May, 1906), 522-523; the *Academy*, LXX (March 3, 1906), 206-207; the *Academy*, LXXIV (March 14, 1908), 555-557; *Westminster Review*, CLXIX (May, 1908), 605-606; the *Athenaeum*, No. 4203 (May 16, 1908), 615; and *Current Literature*, XLIV (June, 1908), 659-662. The American reception of *The Dynasts* is discussed in Carl J. Weber's *Hardy in America: A Study of Hardy and his American Readers* (Waterville, Maine, 1946), pp. 190-194.

4. A study of Granville-Barker's abridgment would be welcome, but the text, now in the Dorset County Museum, has Hardy's forbidding note on the flyleaf, "This abridgement of *The Dynasts*, with the temporary Prologue, Epilogue, and other lines inserted (solely for the stage performance) is not to be published or reproduced at any time. T. H." (Purdy, p. 135.)

5. Rebecca West, "Hardy's *Dynasts* Staged," *New Republic*, I (December 26, 1914), 26.

6. *Later Years*, p. 222.

7. *Friends of a Lifetime: Letters to Sydney Carlyle Cockerell*, ed. Viola Meynell (London, 1940), p. 297. The letter is dated February 24, 1918.

8. *Early Life*, pp. 266-267.

9. C. Lewis Hind, *The Diary of a Looker-on* (New York, 1908), p. 45.

10. T. S. Eliot, *The Sacred Wood* (New York, 1930), p. 66.

11. Samuel Hynes, *The Pattern of Hardy's Poetry* (Chapel Hill, North Carolina, 1956), p. 174.

12. André Castelot's brilliant biography of Napoleon's son, *King of Rome* (New York, 1960), was based on a careful examination of the eight thousand letters in the Archives of Marie Louise, which had been accidentally discovered in 1957. Castelot scrutinized the personality of Marie Louise more closely than Thomas Hardy did, or could; but his conclusions are not significantly different from those implicit in Hardy's characterization. For the most part Castelot is content to let the story tell itself. At one point, however, he quotes a letter which Marie Louise wrote about her son to Mme. de Montebello in September, 1815: "It is by means of his talents, his intelligence and his chivalry that he will have to make a name for himself, since the name he has by birth is an unfortunate one." Castelot adds, "Marie Louise sometimes makes one feel rather sick" (p. 179).

13. Sir Henry Newbolt, *My World as in My Time: Memoirs* (London, 1932), p. 283.

Works Cited

Archer, William, "Real Conversations. Conversation 1.—With Mr. Thomas Hardy," *The Critic*, XXXVIII (April, 1901), 309-318.

Bailey, James Osler, *Thomas Hardy and the Cosmic Mind: A New Reading of The Dynasts* (Chapel Hill, N. C., 1956).

Bailey, John, *The Continuity of Letters* (Oxford, 1923).

Baugh, Albert C., ed., *A Literary History of England* (New York, 1948).

Blunden, Edmund, *Thomas Hardy* (London, 1958).

Boulton, J. T., ed., *A Philosophical Enquiry into the Origin of our Ideas of the Sublime and Beautiful*, by Edmund Burke (London, 1958).

Brennecke, Ernest, Jr., *The Life of Thomas Hardy* (New York, 1925).

Castelot, André, *King of Rome* (New York, 1960).

Chase, Mary Ellen, *Thomas Hardy from Serial to Novel* (Minneapolis, 1927).

Clifford, Emma, "*The Trumpet Major* Notebook and *The Dynasts*," *RES*, VIII (May, 1957), 149-161.

Dale, T. R., "*The Dynasts* and Eduard von Hartmann," *Notes and Queries*, CCVI (March, 1961), 100-101.

Eliot, T. S., *The Sacred Wood* (New York, 1930).

Fairchild, Hoxie N., "The Immediate Source of *The Dynasts*," *PMLA*, LXVII (March, 1952), 43-64.

Firor, Ruth A., *Folkways in Thomas Hardy* (Philadelphia, 1931).

Garwood, Helen, *Thomas Hardy: An Illustration of the Philosophy of Schopenhauer* (Philadelphia, 1911).

Hardy, Evelyn, ed., *Thomas Hardy's Notebooks and Some Letters from Julia Augusta Martin* (London, 1955).

Hardy, Florence Emily, *The Early Life of Thomas Hardy, 1840-1891* (London, 1928).

  The Later Years of Thomas Hardy, 1892-1928 (New York, 1930).

Hardy, Thomas, "Fine Passages in Verse and Prose: Selected by Living Men of Letters," *Fortnightly Review*, XLII (August, 1887), 304.

  "The Profitable Reading of Fiction," *The Forum* (New York, March, 1888), 57-70.

  "Candour in English Fiction," *The New Review*, II (January, 1890), 15-21.

  "The Science of Fiction," *The New Review*, IV (April, 1891), 315-319.

Hickson, Elizabeth Cathcart, *The Versification of Thomas Hardy* (Philadelphia, 1931).

Hind, C. Lewis, *The Diary of a Looker-on* (New York, 1908).

Hynes, Samuel, *The Pattern of Hardy's Poetry* (Chapel Hill, N.C., 1961).

Works Cited

Jaeger, Werner, *Paideia: The Ideals of Greek Culture*, trans. Gilbert Highet (New York, 1945).

Johnson, S. F., "Burke and Hardy," *TLS*, December 7, 1956, p. 731.

Knox, Norman, *The Word "Irony" and Its Context, 1500-1755* (Durham, N.C., 1961).

Lucas, F. L., *Tragedy: Serious Drama in Relation to Aristotle's Poetics* (London, 1957).

Maitland, Frederic William, *The Life and Letters of Leslie Stephen* (New York, 1906).

Meynell, Viola, ed., *Friends of a Lifetime: Letters to Sydney Carlyle Cockerell* (London, 1940).

Monk, Samuel H., *The Sublime* (Ann Arbor, Michigan, 1960).

Newbolt, Sir Henry, *My World as in My Time: Memoirs* (London, 1932).

Paterson, John, *The Making of* The Return of the Native, University of California *English Studies*, XIX (Berkeley, 1960).

Purdy, Richard Little, *Thomas Hardy: A Bibliographical Study* (Oxford, 1954).

Rideout, John G., "Hardy's Last Words on *The Dynasts*," *Colby Mercury*, VI (June 2, 1936), 85-87.

Rutland, William R., *Thomas Hardy: A Study of His Writings and Their Background* (Oxford, 1938).

Slack, Robert C., "The Text of Hardy's *Jude the Obscure*," *Nineteenth-Century Fiction*, XI (March, 1957), 261-275.

Tillyard, E. M. W., *The English Epic and Its Background* (London, 1954).

Van Doren, Mark, *On Great Poems of Western Literature* (New York, 1962).

Weber, Carl J., *The First Hundred Years of Hardy, 1840-1940: A Centenary Bibliography of Hardiana* (Waterville, Maine, 1942).
Hardy and the Lady from Madison Square (Waterville, Maine, 1952).
Hardy of Wessex: His Life and Literary Career (Hamden, Connecticut, 1962).
"Hardy's Copy of Schopenhauer," *Colby Library Quarterly*, IV (November, 1957), 217-224.
"Hardy's Grim Note in *The Return of the Native*," *The Papers of the Bibliographical Society of America*, XXXVI (1942), 37-45.
(editor), *The Letters of Thomas Hardy* (Waterville, Maine, 1954).

West, Rebecca, "Hardy's *Dynasts* Staged," *New Republic*, I (December 26, 1914), 25-26.

Whitmore, Charles E., "Mr. Hardy's *Dynasts* as Tragic Drama," *MLN*, XXXIX (December, 1924), 455-460.

Wilson, Carroll A., *A Descriptive Catalogue of the Grolier Club Centenary Exhibition, 1940, of the Works of Thomas Hardy, O.M.*, Colby College Monograph No. 9.

Wright, Elizabeth Cox, *Metaphor, Sound, and Meaning in Bridges' The Testament of Beauty* (Philadelphia, 1951).

OTHER WORKS OF INTEREST

Bailey, James Osler, "Hardy's Vision of the Self," *SP*, LVI (January, 1959), 74-101.

Cassidy, John A., "The Original Source of Hardy's *Dynasts*," *PMLA*, LXIX (December, 1954), 1085-1100.

Chew, Samuel C., *Thomas Hardy: Poet and Novelist* (New York, 1928).

Chakravarty, Amiya, *The Dynasts and the Post-War Age in Poetry* (London, 1938).

Church, Richard, "Thomas Hardy as Revealed in *The Dynasts*," *EDH*, XXIX (1958), 1-17.

Clifford, Emma, "The Impressionistic View of History in *The Dynasts*," *MLQ*, XXII (March, 1961), 21-31.

Deutsch, Babette, *Poetry in Our Time* (New York, 1952).

Duffin, H. C., *Thomas Hardy: A Study of the Wessex Novels, the Poems, and The Dynasts* (Manchester, 1937).

Fairley, Barker, "Notes on the Form of *The Dynasts*," *PMLA*, XXXIV (September, 1919), 401-415.

Gillet, Louis, "Thomas Hardy," *Revue des Deux Mondes*, XCVIII (February, 1928), 704-705.

Hardy, Emma, *Some Recollections by Emma Hardy, with Notes by Evelyn Hardy. Together with Some Relevant Poems by Thomas Hardy, with Notes by Robert Gittings* (London, 1961).

Hopkins, A. B., "*The Dynasts* and the Course of History," *SAQ*, XLIV (October, 1945), 432-444.

John O' London's Weekly (June 7, 1940). Hardy Centenary Number.

Pinto, Vivian de Sola, *Crisis in English Poetry, 1880-1940* (London, 1951).

Sherman, G. W., "The Influence of London on *The Dynasts*," *PMLA*, LXIII (September, 1948), 1017-1028.

Southern Review, VI (summer, 1940). Hardy Centenary Number.

Southworth, James G., *The Poetry of Thomas Hardy* (New York, 1947).

Stedmond, J. M., "Hardy's *Dynasts* and the 'Mythical Method,'" *English*, XII (spring, 1958), 1-4.

Stewart, Agnes, "*The Dynasts*: A Psychological Interpretation," *English Review*, XXXVIII (May, 1924), 666-680.

Thouless, Priscilla, *Modern Poetic Drama* (Oxford, 1934).

Valakis, Apollo P. D., "The *Moira* of Aeschylus and the Imminent Will of Thomas Hardy," *Classical Journal*, XXI (March, 1926), 431-442. 442.

Van Doren, Mark, "The Poems of Thomas Hardy," *Four Poets on Poetry*, ed. by Don Cameron Allen (Baltimore, 1959), 83-107.

116

OTHER WORKS OF INTEREST

Webster, Harvey Curtis, *On a Darkling Plain: The Art and Thought of Thomas Hardy* (Chicago, 1947).

Weygandt, Cornelius, *The Time of Yeats* (New York, 1937).

Index

Aberdeen University, 20
Ackermann, Rudolph, 42
Adam, in *Paradise Lost*, 68-69; compared to Napoleon in *The Dynasts*, 73-79
Addison, Joseph, 47, 103
"Address to all Ranks and Descriptions of Englishmen," 42
Adventures and Recollections of Colonel Landmann, The, 42
Aeschylus, 21, 22, 35, 72; *Prometheus Bound*, 27
Alberche brook, Spain, 98
Albuera, Spain, 44, 94-95
Alden, H. M., 13
Alexander I, Tsar of Russia, 58, 77, 80-81, 105
Antoinette, Marie, 80
Aristotle, 47
Army Regulations (1801), 42
Arnold, Matthew, "Thyrsis," 33
Athenaeum, 7
Atlantic Monthly, 8
Augustine, Saint, 25
Aulard, F. A., 33
Austerlitz, 56-57, 63, 93
Avignon, 78

Bagehot, Walter, 86
"Bang-up-Locals," 40
Barnes, William, 100
Baudelaire, Charles, 33
Belgravia, 6, 7
Belle Alliance, La, 42
Bentley, John, 41
Beresina, Bridge of the, 44, 59, 95-96
Berlin, University of, 87
Bishop of Wakefield, 14
Blackwood's Magazine, 14
Blake, William, 67
Blomfield, Arthur, 31
Bohn's translations, 21
Borodino, 77, 78, 95
Bossu, 59, 61, 97
Bourbons, the, 80
Brennecke, Ernest, Jr., 23
Brenton, Edward Pelham, *The Naval History of Great Britain, 1783-1822*, 43
British Broadcasting Corporation, 102
Broadley, A. M., 42
Brunswick, Duke Friedrich Wilhelm Ferdinand of, 96
Brussels, 42, 97
Buchanan, Robert, *A Drama of Kings*, 48
Buckley, Theodore A., 27
Burial Service, 30
Burke, Edmund, *A Philosophical Enquiry into the Origin of our Ideas of the Sublime and Beautiful*, 49-65

Byron, George Gordon, 6th Baron, *Childe Harold's Pilgrimage*, 54

Calvin, John, 25
Cambacérès, Jean Jacques Régis, Arch-Chancellor of France, 81
Cambridge University, 13, 21
Campbell, Thomas, 98
Capefigue, Jean Baptiste Honoré Raymond, *L'Europe pendant le Consulate et l'Empire de Napoléon Ier*, 43
Chapman, George, 103
Charleroi, Belgium, 42, 61, 78
Chatto and Windus, 6
Chelsea Hospital, 41
Chew, Samuel C., 89
Chislehurst, England, 41
choric, 104
Cid, The, 103
Clough, Arthur Hugh, 33
Coleridge, Samuel Taylor, 26, 47
Collins, William Wilkie, *The Moonstone*, 1
Colvin, Sidney, 103
Comte, Auguste, 22, 23
Copernicus, Nicolaus, 69
Coquelle, P., *Napoléon et l'Angleterre, 1803-1813*, 43
Cornhill Magazine, 4, 5, 6, 7
Coruña, Spain, 41, 79
Crichton-Browne, James, 22

Daily News, 102
Dante, 103
Darwin, Charles, 22, 23
Davidson, John, 33
Declaration of the Allies, 78
Decrès, Admiral, 76, 105
Derby, Lord, 103
Devastation, 96
Dickens, Charles, 8
Dokhtorof, Russian general, 93
Don Quixote, 103
Dorchester, England, 88
Dorchester Debating and Dramatic Society, 102
Dostoyevsky, Fyodor, 8
Dowson, Ernest, 33
Dubois, the Accoucheur, 77

Egdon Heath, 50
Eliot, George, 5, 16
Eliot, Thomas Stearns, 104; *The Waste Land*, 105
Empress-Mother of Russia, 81
England, Church of, 25
Englishman's Home, An, 87
Ervine, St. John, 103

119